THE BIBLE AND THE MODERN WORLD

THE BIBLE AND THE MODERN WORLD

David J.A. Clines

Sheffield
Phoenix Press

to my BMW* classes
of 1990-91
of 1992-93
of 1994-95
of...

* Bible in the Modern World, that is–not Bayerische Motoren Werke

Copyright © Sheffield Phoenix Press 2005

First published by Sheffield Academic Press 1997
Reprinted with corrections by Sheffield Phoenix Press 2005

Sheffield Phoenix Press Ltd
Department of Biblical Studies, University of Sheffield
Sheffield S10 2TN UK

www.sheffieldphoenix.com

British Library Cataloguing in Publication Data

A catalogue record for this book is available from the British Library

Printed on acid-free paper by Antony Rowe, Eastbourne

ISBN 1-905048-16-5

CONTENTS

PREFACE

I don't offer lectures, these days, not since I gave up teaching biblical studies and determined to teach my students instead. So I was delighted to have the chance to give a real lecture—to a varied and really interesting audience—four nights in a row. For the book, I couldn't bear not to keep the flavour of the real occasion that the Nazarene College in Didsbury, Manchester provided.

I am in no position to speak of the 'modern world' in general, of Seoul and Guatemala City along with Sheffield and Manchester, and so I unashamedly speak of my little world (it is the same big wide world as yours, but from my restricted angle of vision), which I love, the nooks and crannies of it, its idioms and patois, its high culture and its demotic life, and especially the world of books and words with all their magic of register and allusion and rhythm. My modern world is local and parochial, and I cannot write of it if I am not allowed to be particular; but I have tried to explain the allusions that will be unfamiliar outside its confines. How far are trainspotting, Radio Three and W.H. Smith known beyond these shores?, I wondered.

My warmest thanks go to the staff of the Nazarene Theological College, especially its Dean, Kent Brower, and its Principal, Herbert McGonigle, for doing me the honour of their invitation to deliver these Didsbury Lectures in 1993. Their hospitality and enthusiasm made the week of lectures a very special event. As always, I am much indebted to Heather McKay for contributing more excellent ideas, images and analogies to my writing than I can possibly record in the footnotes. And, as the dedication shows, it has been a special pleasure to conceive and write a book interactively with the work of a class—a class moreover that has been more than the sum of its members in any year, but that has developed, through the concept of the book, a kind of corporate personality, even a transcendental identity.

Sheffield
Australia Day, 1995

CORRIGENDA

p. 21, paragraph 1, line 3: delete 'decentering'
p. 36, paragraph 2, line 2: delete 'interpretation: history of'
p. 47, section 4, paragraph 2, line 1: 'three main characteristics'
p. 51, paragraph 4, line 3: 'that of China until very recent times'
p. 52, line 3: after 'Blyton' insert footnote number 37
p. 76, line 15: delete 'under the'
p. 87, paragraph 3, line 9: after '(falsely so-called)' add 'Apostles'
    Creed'
p. 88, paragraph 2, line 10: 'any particular saying ascribed to Jesus'
p. 99, paragraph 2, line 9: 'Genesis 12–36'

Chapter 1

The Bible and the Academy

'What language is the Bible in?', I asked my son. 'This is a trick question', he said, knowing his father and knowing the 'right' answer and knowing I knew he knew the 'right' answer. 'English', he said—which was the right, not the 'right' answer. 'English' is the right answer, I believe, if the question is asked in English, if the questioner's location is Britain—that is, if you are respecting the location of the questioner; 'English' is the right answer also if you are having any regard for the norm, the average, the statistically significant—for there are more Bibles in English (I suppose) than in any other language, more, perhaps, than in every other language put together. Viewed as an object in the modern world, the Bible is, for the most part, an English book. Chinese or Finnish, too, I allow, but only if you happen to be in the right places. Here in Manchester, the Bible is in English. And you can prove it by walking into any W.H. Smith's.[1] 'Do you have a copy of the Bible?', you ask, and quick as a flash comes the reply, 'I'm sorry, sir, but no; we have no actual Bibles here. All we have are translations.' Or is it not rather the case that up and down the country, booksellers are flogging English books to earnest would-be Bible readers, and citizens are cheerfully parting with serious money for English books under the impression they are buying real Bibles?

Is this a deception? I think not.

But in the academy no one ever told me this. I read it in no book. I never heard a lecture that supposed the Bible was anything other than a book written in Hebrew, Aramaic and Greek

---

1.   A chain of stationers and booksellers, to be found in the High Street (= Main Street) of most British cities and towns.

that had been latterly translated into English. In fact, the Academy, the guild of biblical scholars, earn their living and their status from the difficulty of saying in English what the Bible, written in these obscure and dead languages, said in its own mysterious way. It is in their interests to keep on reminding everyone who will listen that the Bible is *not* an English book. But the evidence of our senses is that it is just that.

This question of the language of the Bible is a symbol or paradigm of the way the Bible is viewed in the Academy. Everywhere in the world of scholarship, liberal college and fundamentalist seminary alike, the Bible is viewed as an ancient book, a product of the past, an inheritance, a heritage; it is essentially a book with origins, which can be more or less known—so the common belief goes—and it cannot be understood, so they say, except through reference to the historical circumstances of its composition.

But this course of lectures is on The Bible and the Modern World, and I want to look during this week at what a difference it can make to what we can say about the Bible if we take one simple and, you would have thought, ungainsayable fact into serious account: that the Bible is *in* the modern world, a physical object strewn about the world of today, an in-print book that real live people are reading at this very moment. I want to look, that is, not at the *origins* of the Bible but at its *reception*, not at what its authors may have intended it to mean, but on what its readers take it to mean. I want to look at the Bible functionally, how it is used, what ends it serves—rather than considering what it is in itself (if indeed such language means anything much).

In this lecture, The Bible and the Academy, I want to consider what would happen in the field of academic biblical studies and what would happen in the classroom if we were to regard the Bible as an object in the modern world—which it is, of course. Here are five things that would happen, I suggest:

1.   The focus of interest would shift from the author or the text to the reader.
2.   Readers and their interests, presuppositions and ideologies would become an object of scholarly enquiry.

3. The textuality of the Bible, that is, the fact that it is a text, a product, an object, would be fully recognized.
4. The Bible would be studied as a cultural artifact and not primarily as a religious text that is the property of religious communities.
5. The curriculum of biblical studies would change, not only to allow room for these new approaches, but, more importantly, to enable students of the Bible to see themselves as readers of the Bible, and thus themselves and their own readings as the subject matter of biblical studies.

1. *From Author or Text to Reader*

I start these lectures with the Academy because that is the place I know best, but also because the Academy claims to know about the Bible, to understand how it should be approached, to be the source and arbiter of methodology in biblical study. No doubt the Academy is not very influential in determining how the Bible will in fact be used and read, for everyone with the price of a copy about their person has their own idea about that—and why not? All the same, the Academy is my locus, and the locus of events like this series of lectures, in some way or other; so there is no point in my ignoring it—no possibility of doing so either.

My first point is this: If we are going to take the presence of the Bible in the modern world seriously, the focus of academic biblical study will have to shift from the author (who is dead and therefore not in the modern world—except underground) or the text itself (which is mute, like texts everywhere) to the reader of the text. Not to say that such a change would be an entire novelty. It is in fact a shift in focus that has already been taking place in the last few decades, and that can pretty readily be sketched.[2]

2. I have done so previously, in somewhat different words, in *What Does Eve Do to Help? And Other Readerly Questions to the Old Testament* (Journal for the Study of the Old Testament Supplement Series, 94; Sheffield: JSOT Press, 1990), pp. 9-12. This developmental schema, in which the reader stands at the apogee of a historical process, is not meant to imply that the end of history has been reached. These days, for my part, I am as much concerned

To start at the beginning.

Author

In the beginning was the word, the written word, the word of an author. Our task as readers of biblical texts, so the Academy insists, and so I was taught as a student, was to think the author's thoughts after him, to 'follow' him. The questions I learned to ask were: What did he (it was always he) mean, when did he live, what did he know, what sources did he use, what was his intention? The meaning of the text was always and exclusively what it meant, what it meant to its author. This was the historical-critical approach to the Bible, and there was no other. No matter that this approach was something of a novelty as a way of going about reading biblical texts, if you considered the sweep of Bible reading throughout history generally; no matter either that it seemed a rather antiquarian attitude to the majority of people who actually were engaged at the same moment in reading the very same texts, but outside the Academy. This was the 'proper' way of reading.

There were three things questionable about this author-centred approach. First, this historical-critical method systematically regarded the text as a window through which to scrutinize something other than the text, namely the author, and, by way of him, historical actuality. Now studying the view through windows is an excellent idea, especially if there is no way of getting out into the landscape yourself. But it is not so clever an idea when the window is a magnificent stained glass one, and all there is on the outside is a brick wall, or a fog. And, indeed, it has come more and more to seem that most of what we can know about historical reality in the ancient world does in fact closely resemble a brick wall in a fog. In any case, studying the landscape through

with biblical texts as socio-historical documents as with readers pure and simple (see, for example, 'Why is There a Book of Job, and What Does It Do to You If You Read It?', in *The Book of Job* [ed. W.A.M. Beuken; Bibliotheca Ephemeridum Theologicarum Lovaniensium; Leuven: Leuven University Press/Peeters, 1994], pp. 1-20). But, whatever happens to the current foregrounding of readers, my prediction is that, now that they have been put on the interpretational agenda, readers and readers' interests can never again be ignored.

the window has never been the same thing as studying the window itself, and it was always a bit worrying to pretend you were studying the Bible when really you were studying ancient history. Secondly, the wave of uncertainty, from the late 1960s onward, that was sweeping over all sorts of conclusions about historical actuality, events, sources, literary history, and so on, made you wonder whether the best way of reading texts was to go on asking questions about matters that were deeply unknowable. And thirdly, it became apparent that the very idea of seeking the intention of dead (and, for the most part unidentifiable) biblical authors was a waste of time; we had no access to the intentions of authors apart from the texts they left us, so we could not use the intention of the author as a means for understanding the text.[3]

Text

The obvious move was to shift the focus from the author to the text. Now the subject of study tended to become, not what the author meant to say, but what the text means to say. We could happily get on with the matter of the text and its meaning, and simply bracket out the historical questions, not as illegitimate, but as difficult, unresolvable, and boring. This was a very 1970s thing to do in biblical studies. Names for it were rhetorical criticism, holistic interpretation, the final form of the text, synchronic

---

3.   The term 'intentional fallacy' acquired currency to denote the belief that authors' intentions determine the meaning of texts—though, appropriately enough, such a meaning was not quite the intention of those who coined the phrase (W.K. Wimsatt and M.C. Beardsley, 'The Intentional Fallacy', in W.K. Wimsatt, Jr, with Monroe C. Beardsley, *The Verbal Icon: Studies in the Meaning of Poetry* [Lexington, KY: The University Press of Kentucky, 1954], pp. 3-18; reprinted in, for example, *20th Century Literary Criticism: A Reader* [ed. David Lodge; London: Longman, 1972], pp. 333-45). There are those, of course, who do not accept such a dismissal of authors' intentions; see, for example, E.D. Hirsch, *Validity in Interpretation* (New Haven: Yale University Press, 1967), and for a wide-ranging discussion from many points of view, see W.J.T. Mitchell (ed.), *Against Theory: Literary Studies and the New Pragmatism* (Chicago: University of Chicago Press, 1985), a collection of responses to the radically 'intentionalist' lead essay, 'Against Theory', by Steven Knapp and Walter Benn Michaels (pp. 11-30). See also K.K. Ruthven, *Critical Assumptions* (Cambridge: Cambridge University Press, 1979), ch. 9 'Intended Meanings'.

interpretation, New Criticism, formalism.[4] It involved the study of themes, images, character, plot, style, metaphor, point of view, narrators, and so on. Books with titles like *The Structure of Matthew's Gospel*, *Narrative Art in the Bible* or *The Triumph of Irony in the Book of Judges* announced themselves as text-oriented scholarship.[5] It was an immensely rewarding approach to the Bible, and it enabled us to look again at all our favourite texts with new eyes. There are still vast areas of the biblical text waiting to be explored by this approach.

Among the principal concerns of a text-oriented approach were these: (1) It aimed to establish the meaning of a text by reading the text rather than by asking what the author intended. (2) It emphasized the work as a whole, which involves the elucidation of the whole in relation to its parts and of the parts in relation to the whole. (3) It resisted a romantic view of texts as essentially the 'expression' of an author's personality or genius, or as affording an insight into the psychology of a great thinker or artist. It recognized that texts are entities existing in the world, and deserving of study in their own right, regardless of the circumstances of their composition.

There were faults in this approach too.

1. A certain lack of 'engagement with real life'. If we concentrate upon the text as distinct from the moment of its creation in history, the tendency is for the text to be severed from the past, to be idealized, to be regarded as a free-floating object. And, what is more serious, under cover of this professed preoccupation with the text itself, the critic was still able to slip in any number of his or her own prejudices, especially concerning which texts

4.   Helpful summary accounts of such procedures may be found, for example, in *A Dictionary of Biblical Interpretation* (ed. R.J. Coggins and J.L. Houlden; London: SCM Press, 1990).

5.   I choose the titles almost at random. The details are: David R. Bauer, *The Structure of Matthew's Gospel: A Study in Literary Design* (Journal for the Study of the New Testament Supplement Series, 31; Bible and Literature Series, 15; Sheffield: Almond Press, 1988); Shimon Bar-Efrat, *Narrative Art in the Bible* (Journal for the Study of the Old Testament Supplement Series, 70; Bible and Literature Series, 17; Sheffield: Almond Press, 1989); Lillian R. Klein, *The Triumph of Irony in the Book of Judges* (Journal for the Study of the Old Testament Supplement Series, 68; Bible and Literature Series, 14; Sheffield: Almond Press, 1988).

were worth studying. In English literature, New Criticism often hid right-wing values, while in biblical studies, canonical criticism, for example, which might be seen as a kind of New Criticism, brought with it implicit messages about the authority of the church.

2. Even more serious, focus on the text left out the reader. In the making of meaning, readers have a vital part. It has taken a long time to realize that we cannot say, 'This text is meaningful, but it means nothing to me or you or anyone'. Texts only have meanings when readers make meanings out of them. Now, not everyone wants to allow readers to make up any meaning that comes into their heads. But, on the other hand, more and more people are coming to see that texts themselves do not have meanings that readers then proceed to discover. The making of meaning occurs, in some way, in the interaction of text and reader, at the hinge between language and experience.[6]

Reader

So, in the 1980s, the focus in literary studies came to be on the reader. This is good news for the industry of biblical studies, since there have always been more readers than texts out there, and there are no limits to how much you can study readers—for there are as many readings as readers. Names for this approach are post-structuralism, reader response, political exegesis.[7]

The reality of it is like this: Edward Greenstein, the Jewish biblical scholar, tells of how he handled opposition to this idea and dealt with students who kept claiming that it was our business as readers to suppress our own interests and simply 'listen to the text'.[8] One day he came into the classroom with a Hebrew Bible, laid it on the desk, and announced, 'Today, we are simply going to listen to the text. Today, we shall hear what *it* has to say.' And fell silent. Within five minutes his restless class had come to

---

6.   Kent Harold Richards uses this phrase from Paul Ricoeur in his paper 'From Scripture to Textuality', *Semeia* 40 (1987), pp. 119-24 (121).

7.   Perhaps I can mention just one title in this connection: *The Reader in the Text: Essays on Audience and Interpretation* (ed. Susan R. Suleiman and Inge Crosman; Princeton: Princeton University Press, 1980).

8.   Edward L. Greenstein, *Essays on Biblical Method and Translation* (Atlanta: Scholars Press, 1989).

interesting ✱

realize that texts themselves cannot speak and have nothing to say; without readers, the Bible text, like all texts, is mute.

Talking of texts talking is of course a metaphor; it is not at all foolish, and it has its uses. I shan't normally protest if someone says, 'John 3.16 says, "God so loved the world..."'—or even if they say, 'John 3.16 reads...', as if it were texts that read and not readers. It's when you erect this shorthand into a grand theory about texts speaking for themselves, start attributing intrinsic significance to black marks on white paper, and forget about me and my kind, the readers, the real people who quicken texts to life, that I get upset.

2. *Readers and their Interests*

So what of these readers, then? All readers of biblical texts, as of any texts, are interested readers, even if they are yawning; for they bring their own interests, prejudices and presuppositions with them when they open a text. Now while we would be wrong to insist that the Bible should say what we want it to say, we would be equally wrong to think that it does not matter, in reading the Bible, what we ourselves already believe. For it is the combination of our own interests, values and commitments that makes us persons with identity and integrity; in no activity of life, and certainly not in reading, can we hide or abandon our values without doing violence to our own integrity. If one is, for example, a feminist pacifist vegetarian—which are quite serious things to be, even if they happen to be modish (so is lead-free petrol, but we don't snigger)—it will be important to us to ask what the text has to say, or fails to say, about these issues. We may have to recognize that the text has little concern with such matters, but if they are a serious concern to us they may be legitimately put on the agenda for interpretation, that is, the mutual activity that goes on between text and reader.

interesting

It remains open to us, of course, to read forever in a historical mode, reconstructively reading our way toward a determinate goal of discovering the author's meaning or hypothesizing how the work was heard in its own time—and resting content with that. But alternatively (or, as well), we may approach the text with the reading strategies of our own time, not indeed to corrupt the

✗

how?

text into saying whatever it is we want it to say but to hear whatever it may have to say on matters we are, out of our own convic-
tions and interests, concerned about.

So here is something like a new programme for biblical studies
at the end of the century, a redrawing of the map. If we take the
presence of the Bible in the modern world seriously, and ask what
academic questions we can ask about that state of affairs, we have
to concentrate on what people are making of the Bible, what
reception it is receiving, how it is being understood, what it is
capable of meaning to real live people who are friends and neighbours, enemies and interlocutors. Needless to say, you will go a
long way before you find academic programmes and courses of
study like this, for very few people in our field seem to be interested in what is the case—most are quite wrapped up in what
ought to be the case. Who in the Academy is studying, for example, how the Bible is understood in Pentecostal churches or in the
pages of *The Guardian*?[9] Who is there out there collecting as many
new interpretations of the Bible as possible? Everyone is too busy
finding out (that's what they call it, finding out) and telling us
what the Bible actually does mean—its one and only meaning,
its true meaning, its authentic meaning, its determinate meaning.
This prescriptiveness in biblical studies is all due to the moralism
and the dogmatism of religious believers, no doubt; but it's a bit
of a scandal really that in the academic context it is religious
believers who are setting the tone for the study of the Bible .

If now it is going to be readers who decide what the texts mean,
and if we are going to have lots of readers deciding that the texts
mean lots of things, what we in the Academy should be studying—when we are doing biblical studies—is not so much the
Bible, but readers of the Bible. That is to say, rather than striving
for one determinate meaning that we can agree is *the* meaning of
the text, we should be recognizing, identifying and analysing the
various kinds of meanings the Bible actually has to its very varied readers.

9. Probably the most intellectual and socially aware of daily newspapers in Britain.

This will be the theme of the next three lectures: how the Bible is being read by its various readers, first by the purveyors of culture, then by the public at large, and then by the church.

3. *The Textuality of the Bible*

All texts have two things at least in common: they participate in the inherent unsatisfactoriness of writing, and they are products.[10] These are not, however, angles of vision on the Bible that find a place in normal academic biblical study.

1. Most of us were brought up to believe in the transparency of language, in the fitness of words to represent things, and in the idea of language as a tool, a tool as precise as a screwdriver or a fretsaw. All my schooldays I was being trained to believe that words had exact meanings, and texts had correct meanings, and that it was my business to find them out, turning, with effort of course, Homer into English, Gladstone into Latin, without loss or fuzziness. Being clear, exact, precise, unambiguous in language was not only desirable—it was possible. And the Bible was the supremely transparent text, for it had been modelled by its divine author as a channel of revelation and communication; if any author knew what he was talking about it was God, and if any author cared for precise and accurate communication, it had to be the divine author of the scriptures. As Matthew Arnold put it, there is 'one English book, and one only, where...perfect

---

10. These are not of course the only things that may be said about texts generally. We might, for example, characterize them as discourses fixed in writing. See Robert P. Scharlemann, 'Theological Text', *Semeia* 40 (1987), pp. 6-19 (7-8), for a helpful summary of Paul Ricoeur's views in his 'Qu'est-ce qu'un texte? Expliquer et comprendre', in *Hermeneutik und Dialektik. Aufsätze II. Hans-Georg Gadamer zum 70. Geburtstag* (ed. R. Bubner, K. Cramer and R. Wiehl; Tübingen: J.C.B. Mohr [Paul Siebeck], 1970), pp. 181-200. A text is a displacement of the oral (one writes instead of speaking), it is a burial of the speaker (a book is a testament from an author viewed as already dead, not a conversation with a living interlocutor), it is the replacement of the physical world of objects and of the ostensive world of spoken language by a quasi-world of the text, it is the globalization of the addressee (anyone who can read can become a reader of this text), it is the abandonment of the author's intention as a control for meaning, and so forth.

plainness of speech is allied with perfect nobleness; and that book is the Bible'.[11]

I think it was really Saussure who started us on the slippery slope away from all that, arguing beyond contradiction that language is not a reflection of reality but a system of mutually self-defining elements.[12] Meanings were not properties of words, and words did not 'have' meanings as wallets have banknotes—for words had meanings only in relation to other words, like colours in relation to their place on the spectrum. 'Warm' had no meaning of its own, but only in relation to 'hot' and 'cold'—which in turn had no meaning of their own but only in relation to other words, a hot bath and a hot day being very different in temperature. And words had meaning only in the contexts of sentences, and sentences in the context of discourses. And the connection between the signifying word and the signified object—between the words 'tree', 'arbre' and 'Baum' on the one side and the thing itself—was deeply arbitrary, even if conventional. The upshot was that language was problematized, and its transparency disappeared for ever.

And then the literary critics fell upon the artfulness of language, and its undecidability, on the way language frosts over reality and never really functions as plain glass. In the 60s and 70s we Bible readers began picking up the language of the literary critics, the talk of irony, of ambiguity and of metaphor, and began to recognize that there was an art of biblical narrative, as Robert Alter called it,[13] a reticence, a suggestiveness, an indirection that made texts into delightful and intriguing mysteries rather than merely practical and effective means of communication.

Then the final blow against the 'common sense' view of texts as messages from author to reader came with Jacques Derrida's

11. Matthew Arnold, *On Translating Homer* (1861), ch. 3 (in M. Arnold, *On the Classical Tradition* [ed. R.H. Super; Ann Arbor: University of Michigan Press, 1960], pp. 97-216).

12. Ferdinand de Saussure's key work was his *Cours de linguistique générale*, published originally in 1916 from lecture notes by his students. A standard English translation is: *Course in General Linguistics* (ed. Charles Bally and Albert Sechehaye in collaboration with Albert Reidlinger; London: Fontana, 1974).

13. Robert Alter, *The Art of Biblical Narrative* (London: George Allen & Unwin, 1981). See especially ch. 6, 'Characterization and the Art of Reticence'.

concept of deconstruction: that it is in the nature of texts to carry within them the seeds of their own undermining.[14] Every text, he said, was built on binary oppositions of ideas, and yet every text somehow let drop some hint about the defectiveness of the very systems of oppositions it seemed to promote, thus deconstructing itself. The Book of Job, he might have said, sets out to destroy the dogma of retribution, that it is wickedness that brings suffering and piety that brings reward, but cannot come to an end without deconstructing itself by affirming the dogma and portraying Job as the righteous man who is blessed.[15] Even the twenty-third Psalm lays itself open to deconstruction when the worshipper as sheep is comforted by the thought of returning to, or dwelling in, the Lord's house for ever; for our knowledge of why sheep go to the Lord's temple—their destiny as lamb chops—undermines the image of security the poem has been at such pains to establish.[16]

All these ideas about language—its problematics, its ambiguities and its deconstructability—are twentieth-century ideas, to be sure, but, if they are true (whatever that may mean), they have always been true, even about texts as ancient as the Bible. Such are the natures of texts, and academic readers of the Bible at the end of the twentieth century will have to be recognizing it as a text of those kinds, a text among texts.

2. And texts are products. They are not just the thoughts of their authors, or artistic compositions, or powerful literature. They are produced objects, produced for a readership and sold in the market. They are unique objects, not mass-produced like cat food or toilet tissue, but commodities all the same, and they obey the economic and political laws of producers and consumers as they

14. See, for example, Jonathan Culler, *On Deconstruction: Theory and Criticism after Structuralism* (London: Routledge & Kegan Paul, 1983); Christopher Norris, *Deconstruction: Theory and Practice* (London: Methuen, 1982).

15. This is the theme of my article, 'Deconstructing Job', in *What Does Eve Do to Help? And Other Readerly Questions to the Old Testament* (Journal for the Study of the Old Testament Supplement Series, 94; Sheffield: JSOT Press, 1990), pp. 106-23 (originally published in *The Bible and Rhetoric: Studies in Biblical Persuasion and Credibility* [ed. Martin Warner; London: Routledge, 1990], pp. 65-80).

16. I have explored this theme more fully in 'Varieties of Indeterminacy', in *Textual Indeterminacy, Part Two* (ed. Robert C. Culley and Robert B. Robinson) = *Semeia* 63 (1995), pp. 17-27 .

have existed through the ages. So we will not rightly understand the Bible at the end of our century if we do not recognize it as a text of this very kind. It was Marx who taught us to think of texts as products, of literature as well as many other human institutions as the superstructure on an economic base;[17] and though that is not the whole story about texts, it is one story that hasn't yet percolated into the academic consciousness within the biblical guild. And it was a Marxist critic, Fredric Jameson, who taught us further that the production of a text always implies the prior existence of a social conflict.[18] For who wants the labour of writing if they have no case to argue, no point to make, no corner to fight, no angle to push? And, furthermore, if texts are written out of a context of conflict, they are also written in order to suppress, or repress, that conflict. Texts are written on paper, and, like paper of all kinds, the paper of texts is useful for pasting over cracks, cracks in the social fabric.

Reading biblical texts, then, is not just work for the hermeneut, the literary critic or the theologian; it cannot be simply a matter of understanding the meaning, appreciating the ideas, or panning for theological paydirt. Reading obliges us also to inferences about the historical matrix of the texts' composition. Which social group's interests are represented by the Ten Commandments?, we find ourselves asking, and, Why are they portraying their society as a community of equal 'neighbours', respecting one another's property, when plainly there were many members of the society, women, aliens, slaves, who were *not* neighbours?[19] What

17. See, for example, Terry Eagleton, *Marxism and Literary Criticism* (London: Methuen, 1976); D.W. Fokkema and Elrud Kunne-Ibsch, *Theories of Literature in the Twentieth Century* (London: C. Hurst & Co., 1978), ch. 4 'Marxist Theories of Literature'.

18. Fredric Jameson, *The Political Unconscious: Narrative as a Socially Symbolic Act* (London: Methuen, 1981). I have developed this idea more fully in 'Haggai's Temple, Constructed, Deconstructed and Reconstructed', *Scandinavian Journal of the Old Testament* 7 (1993), pp. 19-30 (also in *Second Temple Studies* [ed. Tamara C. Eskenazi and Kent H. Richards; Journal for the Study of the Old Testament Supplement Series; Sheffield: JSOT Press, 1993], pp. 51-78).

19. This is the question I address in 'The Ten Commandments, Reading from Left to Right', in *Words Remembered, Texts Renewed: Essays in Honour of John F.A. Sawyer* (ed. Jon Davies, Graham Harvey and Wilfred G.E. Watson;

happens to the piety of the Psalms, we find ourselves asking, if we regard them as the bespoke products of religious fat cats who have created the sacrificial system in their own interests—or as the unconscious reflections of an exclusively masculine world-view?[20] And so on, neverendingly.

4. *The Bible as Cultural Artifact*

I referred to this aspect of the Bible already when I took you to W.H. Smith's in the High Street. And it will be a theme of the next two lectures, on the Bible in high culture and the Bible in popular culture. Here I am thinking exclusively of the academic response to this reality: that the Bible is an artifact of our culture.

What I mean by that is that it is not the property of some group within the culture. It is not owned by the church or the synagogue, for example. I am wanting to conceive ownership in a primarily economic sense, and to argue that it is ownership in this sense that gives the right of use. If I use my copy of the Bible, for which I have paid my own money, to prop up a chair, that is my business, and no one has the right to tell me I should not do that or that that is not what the Bible is 'for'. And if a Bible reader tells me that he finds the most comforting verse in the Bible to be 'and it came to pass',[21] it is not for me to say that it is not comforting, or that he has no right to read it that way.

Now where this matter of the ownership of the Bible impinges on the Academy is—not to put too fine a point on it—the question whether the church should determine what the Academy does

Journal for the Study of the Old Testament Supplement Series, 195; Sheffield: Sheffield Academic Press, 1995), pp. 97-112 (reprinted in my *Interested Parties: The Ideology of Writers and Readers of the Hebrew Bible* [Journal for the Study of the Old Testament Supplement Series, 205; Gender, Culture, Theory, 1; Sheffield; Sheffield Academic Press, 1995], pp. 26-45).

20. The latter is the theme of my paper, 'The Book of Psalms, where Men are Men… On the Gender of Hebrew Piety' (a preliminary version is available at www.shef.ac.uk/uni/academic/A-C/biblst/).

21. The Bible reader in this traditional story is usually a woman, a 'little old lady' who, of course, knows nothing of scientific exegesis. In affirming her right to read the Bible for herself, I have immasculated her, I know (Esther Fuchs's term); but it is my way, as a male, of identifying myself with her position as subject.

with the Bible, and whether the Academy should care whether the church likes what it is doing with the Bible or not. As far as I can see, it is only the church that seriously threatens to encroach on the Academy's use of the Bible—not, for example, the state or the film industry—and so it is the church that the Academy is resisting when it declares the Bible to be public property, to be an artifact of our culture.

What is the Academy to be doing with cultural artifacts, then? What is the appropriate academic attitude to a cultural object like the Bible? Now the Academy is not in the business of preserving or collecting or displaying—it is not a museum or an art gallery. Nor is it in the business of advertising or promoting or persuading—it is not a commercial company or a political party. It is in the business of analysing, critiquing and evaluating. That is its unique social role, and if it doesn't carry out that role there is no one in the society who will. We need academic departments of pharmacology that will check out new drugs free of the commercial pressures of the drug companies, politics departments that will analyse what is happening in Britain without suspicion of the influence of the political parties, and theology departments that will test to destruction new theological ideas before they are unleashed on an unsuspecting public.

But when it comes to biblical studies, the whole subject seems to have been the victim of a huge deception. Not one academic biblical scholar in a hundred will tell you that their primary task is to *critique* the Bible. For some reason, we have convinced ourselves that our business is simply to *understand*, to *interpret*. Here we have some difficult texts from the ancient world, we say, rightly enough. Do you want to know what they *mean*? Then come to us, we are the experts, we *understand* them, we shall tell you how to *interpret* them. But don't ask us for *evaluation*, for *critique*. Oh no, we are objective scholars, and we prefer to keep hidden our personal preferences and our ethical and religious views about the subject matter of our study. Never ask a New Testament scholar for his or her own views on Christology, I long ago learned. It is bad form.

But merely *understanding* hot potatoes like the Bible is wimpish, I think. What the world needs to know, what academic biblical scholars are being paid public money by the state for, are answers to the questions: Is there any truth in this stuff? If there is, what kind of truth is it? And if there is falsity, is it doing anyone any harm? And should we go on supporting this enquiry out of the national exchequer?

Biblical scholars, being modest folk, throw up their hands in horror at the thought of being responsible for answering questions like these. But if they don't, who will? Who is there to deal with such questions who has any chance of seeming unprejudiced and non-partisan? Why does Channel 4 ask Peter Franks from the Department of Politics at the University of Essex for his opinions on what is happening in Russia? Not just because he happens to know a lot about it, for there must be hundreds of Russians who know a good deal more than he does. It's because his social location—in the Academy—is some guarantee of his fairminded and non-partisan evaluation of new events that we non-professionals have seen with our own eyes. If we had to depend on our politicians and theirs to evaluate what was happening, we should soon despair of knowing anything at all.

But it's not just a practical question of our sponsors and our public getting the evaluations they need. It's an ethical one—an ethical question for the professionals in biblical studies themselves.[22] The question is whether it is moral to restrict one's scholarly concern to mere understanding when the subject matter is offensive or questionable to oneself. No one thinks an objective seminar on the feasibility of making lampshades out of human skin is an ethical possibility. Is it then ethically possible to discuss the role of women in patriarchal societies like the world of the Bible without making at the same time one's own evaluation of the texts that represent that situation? Is it ethical to discuss the

22. On this question I found very stimulating the article by Steve Fowl, 'The Ethics of Interpretation; or, What's Left Over after the Elimination of Meaning', in *The Bible in Three Dimensions: Essays in Celebration of the Fortieth Anniversary of the Department of Biblical Studies, University of Sheffield* (ed. David J.A. Clines, Stephen E. Fowl and Stanley E. Porter; Journal for the Study of the Old Testament Supplement Series, 87; Sheffield: JSOT Press, 1990), pp. 379-98. In my view he takes the discussion well beyond the point reached by Elisabeth Schüssler Fiorenza in her important 1987 Society of Biblical Literature presidential address, 'The Ethics of Interpretation: Decentering Biblical Scholarship', published in *Journal of Biblical Literature* 107 (1988), pp. 101-15.

theme of sin and punishment in the prophets without introjecting one's own best ideas on disciplining children, handling problem colleagues, reforming the prison system and abolishing capital punishment? So long as evaluation is not prejudice, is there anything that should not be evaluated? And if you ask, Evaluated according to what norm?, there is no special difficulty; for there are (in my book) no absolutes, no universal standards, and so there is nothing wrong with using your own standards. Not only is there nothing wrong, nothing else would be right; for 'ethical' can only mean 'ethical according to me and people who think like me', and if I don't make judgments according to my own standards, according to whose standards shall I be making them, and in what sense could those judgments be *mine*?

What it boils down to is this: To be truly academic, and worthy of its place in the Academy, biblical studies has to be truly critical, critical not just about lower-order questions like the authorship of the biblical books or the historicity of the biblical narratives, but critical about the Bible's contents, its theology, its ideology. And that is what biblical studies has notoriously not been critical about at all.[23] To be critical, you have to take up a standard of reference outside the material you are critiquing;[24] but, traditionally, biblical scholars have been believers, ecclesiastics or, at the least, fellow-travellers and sympathizers with the ideology of the Bible. When the academy begins to view the Bible as a cultural artifact, and is not seduced or pressured by religious commitments, the hallmark of its criticism will be that it steps outside the ideology of the text.[25]

23. Nor literary critics who write about the Bible, for the most part. These days, they don't write like J.H. Gardiner, assistant professor of English at Harvard in 1906, and author of *The Bible as English Literature* (London: T. Fisher Unwin, 1906): 'It is obvious … that no literary criticism of the Bible could hope for success which was not reverent in tone. A critic who should approach it superciliously or arrogantly would miss all that has given the book its power as literature and its lasting and universal appeal' (p. vii). But they're all mightily respectful, Harold Bloom, Frank Kermode, Gabriel Josopovici, Robert Alter, and all.

24. My colleague Philip Davies gave me this crucial idea.

25. I learned this important phrase, and what it stands for, from my colleague J. Cheryl Exum, who has developed her feminist criticism of the Hebrew Bible under its aegis; see, for example, her *Fragmented Women:*

What will such a criticism look like? I take as an example the case of the prophet Amos. There may be a critical book written about Amos, but, if so, I have never seen it. All the books simply take Amos's point of view for granted. Amos is right, his opponents are wrong; Amos is fair; Amos is accurate; Amos is immensely perceptive; Amos is inspired.[26] All this may be true; but to *assume* it is simply not critical, not academic.

Here is a striking example of commentators' incapacity to think critically. In the introduction to the massive Anchor Bible commentary on Amos by Andersen and Freedman they have a section on 'The God of Israel in the Book of Amos'. It opens by saying:

> Our purpose is to present Amos' picture of the deity, not ours, and to keep it within the thought world of the ancient Near East and the Bible rather than to translate it into contemporary theological or philosophical language.[27]

That is a claim to objective scholarship; and so far, so good. But by the time the section is concluding, we find them saying:

> What it finally comes down to is the nature of the God of the Bible, the person with whom the prophet must deal (and vice versa) and the person around whom everything turns. When all of the superlatives have been exhausted and when all of the authority or majesty have been accorded and the recognition given to the one incomparable deity who stands uniquely alone and against everything that is perishable, vulnerable, corruptible, and the rest, he nevertheless remains a person. That is the fundamental and ultimate category in the Bible, as without it nothing else matters... Once it is agreed that this God—creator and sustainer of heaven and earth, sole and unique—is the God of the Bible and Israel and

Feminist (Sub)versions of Biblical Narratives (Journal for the Study of the Old Testament Supplement Series, 16; Sheffield: JSOT Press, 1993).

26. Here I am drawing upon my paper, 'Metacommentating Amos', in *Of Prophets' Visions and the Wisdom of Sages: Essays in Honour of R. Norman Whybray on his Seventieth Birthday* (ed. Heather A. McKay and David J.A. Clines; Journal for the Study of the Old Testament Supplement Series, 162; Sheffield: JSOT Press, 1993), pp. 142-60.

27. Francis I. Andersen and David Noel Freedman, *Amos: A New Translation with Introduction and Commentary* (Anchor Bible, 24A; Garden City, NY: Doubleday, 1989), p. 88.

Amos and the rest of us, then we may draw closer and ask him
who he is, what he is like, and how things run in this world.[28]

By this point, plainly, we readers are not reading any more about
Amos and the ancient world, for Amos had no Bible and thus no
God of the Bible. Nor are we reading about Amos's God when
we read that God is 'against everything that is perishable, vulner-
able, corruptible'—for are those terms not true of humanity, and
is Amos's God 'against' humanity in general? And when, at the
end, we start to read about what is 'agreed' and told that 'we'
may 'draw closer and ask him who he is' (how?), we can feel sure
that the authors' trumpeted scholarly interests in the ancient
world have been submerged by their own ideological beliefs.

To take another example, Amos himself (the character Amos in
the book by that name, I mean) believes in punishment. He believes in punishment, lots of it, for every sort of crime and mis-
demeanour, from war crimes to race hatred, from disobeying prophetic words to banqueting. He believes that punishment should
be capital. And he believes that capital punishment is what his
nation deserves and what its god will mete out to it. Most of us
in the modern world, on the other hand, feel that we have quite a
few options open to us when we see wrong being committed or
when we ourselves are wronged by someone else, and that inflict-
ing injury on others is either a raw instinctive and immediate
impulse or else a cruel cold-blooded decision we come to at the
end of our tether, and then feel guilty about, but try to justify
nevertheless on some rational grounds. Revenge and punishment are complicated matters for us, but they aren't for Amos.
Everything is straightforward in his accounting. Then when we
become readers of the powerful and indignant—and hugely persuasive—prophecies of Amos, are we going to abandon our moral
repertory, with its sensitivities and its uncertainties, which we
have acquired personally and collectively at some cost, and
accede to the simple moral defeatism of an outraged prophet?

It is not for the Academy to tell people what they should do,
and anyone who wants to resist the implications I have been
drawing is free to do so. But let us all be clear about what is going
on. If the church, or believers, want to submit to the moral dictates

28. Andersen and Freedman, *Amos*, p. 97.

of a book they believe to be the word of God to them, they have every right to do so. But submission is the name for it; that is what they are doing, and it is precisely the Academy's business to point out that that is what they are doing, for no one else is going to. If some of us want to privilege the Bible as a norm for life, no one has the right to stop us. But you will not be surprised, I hope, if the Academy takes it into its head to draw attention to the way in which this cultural artifact, the Bible, is being used, and offer its own evaluations of the likely outcome of such a process.

5. *The Bible in the Classroom*

What I have been presenting is essentially a postmodern agenda for biblical studies. Notions of authority, absolutes, determinacy have been decentering decentred or reconceived, and pluralism is the order of the day.[29] Compared with modernism, the prevalent worldview of our century, in the postmodern ideology people matter more, because if there are no absolutes, people cannot be expected to bend to them. Meaning matters too, but not some one right meaning (because there is no such thing), but everyone's meanings (for that is all there is). Ethics matters more, because we recognize that we are all responsible for the effects of our scholarship (which was not the case, for example, even with the inventors of the atom bomb). The tradition of scholarship does not matter very much, because the tradition enshrined and promoted the principles common to both dogmatic and modernist scholarship, the principles of a unified truth and a common

29. The postmodern turn, as it has been called (notably by Ihab Hassan, *The Postmodern Turn: Essays in Postmodern Theory and Culture* [Columbus, OH: Ohio State University Press, 1987]), is sketched in works like Brenda K. Marshall, *Teaching the Postmodern: Fiction and Theory* (New York: Routledge, 1992); Hans Bertens, *The Idea of the Postmodern: A History* (London: Routledge, 1995). A fundamental text is Jean-François Lyotard, *The Postmodern Condition: A Report on Knowledge* (trans. Geoff Bennington and Brian Massumi; Theory and History of Literature, 10; Minneapolis: University of Minnesota Press, 1984). Cf. also Edgar V. McKnight, *Postmodern Use of the Bible: The Emergence of Reader-Oriented Criticism* (Nashville: Abingdon Press, 1988); Walter Brueggemann, *The Bible and Postmodern Imagination: Texts under Negotiation* (London: SCM Press, 1993).

quest for that truth that we were all engaged in—and 'grand narratives'[30] like that no longer carry conviction.

Now the classroom is the testbed for such an agenda. It is interesting how well the agenda for the discipline of biblical studies as I have been propounding it lines up with currents in educational thinking and praxis that are shaping our lives as teachers. I offer a few thoughts about the Bible in the classroom under some slogans.

a. *Skills and knowledge.* In the postmodern classroom, skills are more important than knowledge. Education is not the absorbing of facts, which will in any case be out of date in five or ten years' time, even if they have not been forgotten in five or ten minutes after the exam, but the acquisition of skills that will be transferable to other subjects and that will prove as hard to forget as knowing how to ride a bicycle. My aim in the classroom these postmodern days is to teach nothing to my students they can possibly forget. I don't just mean practical skills like using MacBible or the ATLA database,[31] but intellectual skills of evaluation and critique, of analysis from varying points of view, of exposing hidden ideologies. These are the skills in biblical studies our students need to learn, even more than Greek and Hebrew, and certainly more than form criticism or the synoptic problem.

b. *Task and process.* Like skills versus knowledge, this is another binary opposition, in this case privileging 'process'. The efficient, male model of learning is to focus on task, and operate with metaphors of conquest of the subject matter. But it is hard with this model to understand why blockages in learning occur, or to transfer the learning methods acquired in one subject to another subject. Focusing on process brings to the surface the emotional

30. The term is Lyotard's; see *The Postmodern Condition*, esp. pp. 31-41.
31. MacBible is computer software enabling you to search any one of a number of English versions of the Bible (or the Hebrew or Greek originals) for the occurrences of a word or a phrase. You can, for example, ask to see all the places where Abraham and Sarah appear in the same verse, or all the places where Paul, apostle and servant appear within three verses of one another. The ATLA (American Theological Library Association) database is a CD-ROM of bibliographical data about scholarly books and articles in religion since about 1960. You can search for a biblical person, a theological term or a biblical reference; you would find some hundreds of references for a term like 'postmodern'.

components of learning, identifies the barriers to learning, and involves the whole person in the learning cycle. Since the subject matter is not the text 'out there' but the interaction of the reader with the text, readers' reflections on what is happening to them become part of the subject of study.[32]

c. *Students' responsibility for their own learning.* When the teacher is no longer the authority but more the resource person, students' goals cannot be to please the teacher or meet the teacher's demands, but they themselves have to take the learning process into their own hands, and make of it what is most suitable for themselves. Their backgrounds and their needs have to help to shape the curriculum.

d. *The student as reader.* Since biblical study is about readings of texts, and a classroom is made up of different readers, the classroom can become a laboratory for experimenting with and evaluating readings.

e. *The student as teacher.* If it is true that we remember 10% of what we read, 20% of what we hear, 30% of what we see, 50% of what we see and hear, 70% of what we say, and 90% of what we say as we do something, then the most successful forms of learning are likely to be those where students explain to others what they know.

I can therefore expect you to remember only 20% of this lecture. But if I now split you in groups to discuss certain points, or required you to give a three-minute account of it tomorrow to somebody (anybody), you might improve your retention rate threefold. In any case, I shall know that whatever you feel is important enough to talk about will be what this hour of your time has gained for you; and that if you take home no seedcorn to sow and reap threefold by tomorrow at 7, you will vote with your feet and watch the box instead.

---

32. I have tried to bring the distinction between task and process into the foreground in a report I wrote of a workshop at the joint meeting of the Society for Old Testament Study and the Oudtestamentische Werkgezelschap, in Kampen, The Netherlands ('Beyond Synchronic/ Diachronic', in Johannes C. de Moor (ed.), *Synchronic or Diachronic? A Debate on Method in Old Testament Exegesis* [Oudtestamentische Studiën, 34; Leiden: Brill, 1995], pp. 52-71).

Chapter 2

THE BIBLE AND CULTURE

In the previous lecture, on the Bible and the Academy, I spoke of the Bible as a cultural artifact in the modern world, and asked how the Academy might treat it if it recognized it in this way, and not just as an object from the ancient world. Today I want to focus on the term 'cultural' and attempt to identify what role the Bible actually plays in our culture. I am using 'culture' in the sense of 'high culture' or 'art culture', because in tomorrow's lecture, on the Bible and the public, I want to deal with the question of how the Bible is perceived in more popular culture. But, I admit, it isn't always easy to know where high culture ends and popular culture begins.

There is quite a lot of extravagant stuff talked about the Bible and culture, because the people who write about the subject always seem to want to maximize the effect the Bible has had on culture and the role it plays in our culture of the present. And there is an awful lot of 'golly gosh' about it too, because people get excited when they find biblical allusions in Shakespeare or Philip Larkin. You can't blame them, because that's what they were looking for, and it's always nice to know you're not wasting your time. But still, there's more than a touch of the trainspotter[1] about collectors of data on the Bible and culture.

In this lecture I certainly want to do some trainspotting, because we need to have some factual data about how the Bible is being used in our culture before we can generalize about the subject, and the data are not easily identifiable. But I do want to

---

1. Trainspotting is an activity engaged in primarily by prepubescent boys; it consists of spending long hours on railway stations or beside railway lines collecting the numbers of passing locomotives and arranging them in lists.

go a lot further than collecting data, and to draw some conclusions. These are the questions I want to ask:

1.   Why are we interested in the question of the role of the
      Bible in culture anyway?
2.   Does the Bible have a big influence on the culture or a
      little?
3.   Where, in the culture, does that influence mainly lie?
4.   What happens to the Bible when it is used in a general
      cultural context? Is that good for the Bible or bad?
5.   Is the Bible, in the way it is used, good for the culture or
      bad?

But a few definitions first.

What is 'culture in the modern world'? What I mean by that
phrase is: the literature, art and music that is available to us in
the modern world. I do not mean just what is being produced in
the modern world. I am in my antihistorical mode today, and just
as I call the Bible an object in the modern world because you can
buy it in W.H. Smith's, I call Rembrandt's paintings of Susanna
and the Elders art in the modern world because you can see them
in Berlin or The Hague, and Bach's *St Matthew Passion* music of
the modern world because you can buy a CD of it.

And what is the 'Bible' that is being referred to as inspiring or
influencing these cultural products? That is a harder question. It
is easy enough if there is a retelling of a biblical story, like that of
Esther in Handel's oratorio of that name, but what if there is an
allusion to a biblical text or a quotation of it 'out of context', as we
might say? And, more difficult still, what of the very idea of God,
of the concept of history as having a purpose, of the notion of a
past golden age of innocence? The Bible has undoubtedly had a
great deal to do with ideas such as these, but who can pinpoint
where it is the Bible's influence at work and not that of Christian
theology or classical culture or Western philosophy? It seems a
hopeless task to try to disentangle the strands, at least without a
lot of specialist and detailed work. But it is just the large issues
like this, and not the trivial and isolated references to biblical
details, that are the most interesting and important; so any such
undertaking as our present one is bound to be frustrating to some

degree, and unscientific, certainly. We can only see what will happen if we start asking the questions.

Let us start with a test case, not from high culture, but as an example of what we can say about the place of the Bible in the modern world.

A few months ago, there was an advertisement in the press and on hoardings (billboards) for a brand of cider called Autumn Gold;.The illustration showed the naked torsos of a male and female side by side, decently screened by two cans of Autumn Gold. The caption ran: IF ONLY THEY HAD WAITED FOR AUTUMN. I turned this advertisement over to my class on The Bible in the Modern World for their exegetical endeavours. They immediately decided that the advertisement would not be intelligible if you did not see the intertextual reference to Adam and Eve. So our first conclusion was that the manufacturers and the advertisers were trading on the fact that the biblical story of Adam and Eve was known to the general public, or at least to its cider-drinking market segment.

But what was it about the illustration that pointed so unmistakably to the Adam and Eve story, and what, furthermore, was the meaning of the caption? It was surely not the nakedness of the couple that told us that it was Adam and Eve, since naked couples are two a penny these days; nor can it have been the fact that they were faceless, for Adam and Eve always have faces, iconographically speaking. Nor was there any garden in the background, as far as I can remember. There was simply the pose of their covering themselves, with hand-held cider cans, alias fig-leaves. That was the clue. But, interestingly, that pose is precisely something that is *not* in the biblical story; that is a purely conventional and traditional portrayal of our first ancestors. In Genesis, they make for themselves 'aprons' of fig-leaves (*culottes* in the Geneva Bible of 1560), which can presumably be worn in some comfort, leaving the hands free for other interesting and useful occupations. So the reference of the advertisement is not strictly to the biblical text, but to conventional representations of the biblical narrative in art.[2] It was an *indirect* use of the Bible.

2. The earliest such representation—of Adam and Eve actually *holding* their fig leaves in front of them—that I have noticed is in the ninth-century

And what did the caption mean? There was no apple in the picture, but we supposed, in the class, that we were meant to draw a
connection between apples and cider—and perhaps, now that we
are all more or less mid-atlantic persons, a connection between
the autumn and the fall (Fall). But what connection, exactly? If
they had waited till autumn, when the apple was ripe, then they
could have drunk cider instead of eating the apple, and that
would not have been a sin? It was rather confusing. But one
thing was certain: that 'if only' was undoubtedly a token of wist-
fulness. Did it mean that if only they had not taken the forbidden
fruit, we should all have been running around Eden still in naked
innocence, enlivened by the odd can of Autumn Gold? It was
hard to be sure. But, whatever exactly it meant, the interesting
thing was that the poster was still not a representation of the biblical story, for there is no *apple* in Genesis 2–3. Where the apple
came from, no one knows, it so happens. Perhaps it was the connection of the apple with love in the Song of Songs (2.5) that
brought it into the Eden story as the path to sexual knowledge;
perhaps there was in early Christianity a confusion between the
Latin *malum* 'apple' and *malum* 'evil'—but in what text?, I wonder.[3] And then there is a further question: What about sex? There
must surely be some sexual allusion in the advertisement; but
what is it? Some wag in the class suggested that if they had waited for Autumn Gold to come on the market they would probably
have become too drunk to have sex, and then the fall wouldn't
have happened. But of course in the biblical story sexual experience comes after the 'fall', and it is not its cause. It's only in

Alcuin Bible, but thereafter it is amply attested in mediaeval art. I see, for
example, Adam and Eve clasping a single fig-leaf each as they are driven
from the garden, in the thirteenth-century Pierpont Morgan miniatures (*Old
Testament Miniatures: A Medieval Picture Book with 283 Paintings from The
Creation to The Story of David* [Introduction and Legends by Sydney C.
Cockerell; New York: George Braziller, n.d.], fol. 2 recto). In some cases, as
in the twelfth-century capital of the church of Saint Martin d'Ainay, Lyons,
they hide their faces with their hands (Louis Réau, *Iconographie de l'art
chrétien.* Tome II. *Iconographie de la Bible.* I. *Ancien Testament* [Paris: Presses
Universitaires de France, 1956], p. 87).
   3.   See, for example, G.L. Scheper, 'Apple', in *A Dictionary of Biblical Tradition in English Literature* (ed. David Lyle Jeffrey; Grand Rapids: Eerdmans,
1992), pp. 49-52 (50).

popular consciousness that the forbidden fruit is identified with sex. Perhaps it means that if they had sampled Autumn Gold they wouldn't have had the inhibitions of Adam and Eve; in that case the whole advertisement may be read as a protest against the puritanical mentality of the traditional biblical story. Who knows?

Putting it all together, what can we say has happened to the Bible in the modern world? In this example, the apron of fig leaves has been cut down to a single fig-leaf, the forbidden fruit has metamorphosed into an apple, and sex has probably become the interpretative key to a text that was earlier nothing to do with sex, but about divine constraints on human desires for life, wisdom and delight. But it is still the Bible! Without the biblical story, the advertisement could not be read and the advertisers would have wasted a lot of money. Genesis 3 obviously still has some of its ancient potency about it, and the Bible is obviously embedded in the culture, even if it is not the Bible academics or churchgoers would recognize.

1. *Collecting the Data about the Bible and Culture*

There are not many sources of data for this subject. The reason is, I believe, that the academic study of the Bible has been essentially antiquarian in cast, and it has not been accepted that the study of the reception of the Bible is a proper and necessary part of biblical study. While the prehistory of the texts has been studied *ad infinitum*, even *ad nauseam*, the posthistory of the texts, their afterlife or *Nachleben*, has rarely been investigated. That situation is no doubt an instance of the romantic quest for origins, as well as of the traditional invisibility of the reader. Now that today's readers are firmly on the agenda for interpretation, yesterday's readers have some chance of recognition too.

Several streams of thinking converge at this point, to help with a theoretical model of what this research about readers living and dead may be. I can mention first the study of reception theory (German *Rezeptionsästhetik*) developed first in the University of Konstanz and associated especially with Wolfgang Iser and Hans Robert Jauss.[4] While reception theory refers strictly to the view

4.   Perhaps its most famous statement lay in the article of Hans Robert

that a literary work should be studied in terms of the effects it has had on those contemporary with its publication, it carries along with it, in a sort of penumbra, an authorization for attending to the end-users of literary works and not principally to authors when we are enquiring about meaning and significance.

Secondly, there is the impact of reader-response criticism, connected with the names of Stanley Fish,[5] Norman Holland[6] and Wolfgang Iser.[7] If, as reader-response criticism argues, the meaning of a literary work lies not in itself but in its readers—as I was arguing yesterday in the first lecture—then exploring the ways readers have read, professional and amateur readers alike, is all grist to the critical mill.

Thirdly, there is the long-established scholarly discipline of the interpretation: history of history of interpretation. In itself, its interests have primarily lain in tracing the development or changes in the way biblical texts have been interpreted through the centuries, or in explaining the variations in biblical interpretation according to the prevailing ethos of the interpreter's own time. But once we recognize prior interpretations of our texts as having more than antiquarian value, and as potentially offering fresh insights into meaning, the whole discipline can be reconceived not as a history of interpretation but as a science of comparative interpretation, in which all the extant interpretations ever offered become part of the concern of the biblical critic.[8]

Jauss, 'Literary History as a Challenge to Literary Theory', *New Literary History* 2 (1970), pp. 7-38.

5.   Stanley Fish, *Is There a Text in This Class? The Authority of Interpretive Communities* (Cambridge, MA: Harvard University Press, 1980).

6.   Norman Holland, *The Dynamics of Literary Response* (Oxford: Oxford University Press, 1968).

7.   Wolfgang Iser, *The Act of Reading: A Theory of Aesthetic Response* (London: Routledge & Kegan Paul, 1976).

8.   On this discipline of the history of interpretation, see, for example, J.F.A. Sawyer, 'Interpretation, History of', in *A Dictionary of Biblical Interpretation* (ed. R.J. Coggins and J.L. Houlden; London: SCM Press, 1990), pp. 316-20. An important innovation in biblical criticism in recent decades has been the stress on the history of exegesis given by Brevard S. Childs, for example in his *Introduction to the Old Testament as Scripture* (London: SCM Press, 1979). I have sketched what I mean by 'comparative interpretation' in 'Possibilities and Priorities of Biblical Interpretation in an International

Fourthly, there is the 'heritage industry', which has nothing directly to do with biblical studies, and not even with literature generally. But I would like to associate with the concept of 'heritage' the current plethora of works of summary and appraisal, reclaiming the scholarly past and evaluating it. Perhaps this movement has something to do with the approaching end of the century. It certainly is an international phenomenon, and not peculiar to this country. I think especially of a series of six volumes commissioned for the 1980 centenary of the American Society of Biblical Literature. They were entitled *The Bible and Bibles in America, The Bible and Popular Culture in America, The Bible and American Arts and Letters, The Bible in American Law, Politics, and Political Rhetoric, The Bible in American Education,* and *The Bible and Social Reform.* [9] Each volume consists of essays by various authors, sometimes rather impressionistic and unsystematic, as is understandable given the conception of the enterprise. But I did find, for example, the best list I have ever seen of operas on

Perspective', *Biblical Interpretation. A Journal of Contemporary Approaches* 1 (1993), pp. 67-87, and in 'A World Founded on Water (Psalm 24): Reader Response, Deconstruction and Bespoke Interpretation', in J. Cheryl Exum and David J.A. Clines (eds.), *The New Literary Criticism and the Hebrew Bible* (Journal for the Study of the Old Testament Supplement Series; Sheffield: JSOT Press, 1993), pp. 79-90. See also David J.A. Clines and Tamara C. Eskenazi (eds.), *Telling Queen Michal's Story: An Experiment in Comparative Interpretation* (Journal for the Study of the Old Testament Supplement Series, 119; Sheffield: JSOT Press, 1991).

9.　　Ernest S. Frerichs (ed.), *The Bible and Bibles in America* (The Bible in American Culture, 1; Atlanta: Scholars Press, 1988), Allene Stuart Phy (ed.), *The Bible and Popular Culture in America* (The Bible in American Culture, 3; Philadelphia: Fortress Press; Chico, CA: Scholars Press, 1985), Giles Gunn (ed.), *The Bible and American Arts and Letters* (The Bible in American Culture, 4; Philadelphia: Fortress Press; Chico, CA: Scholars Press, 1983), James Turner Johnson (ed.), *The Bible in American Law, Politics, and Political Rhetoric* (The Bible in American Culture, 2; Philadelphia: Fortress Press; Chico, CA: Scholars Press, 1985), David Barr and Nicholas Piediscalzi (eds.), *The Bible in American Education: From Sourcebook to Textbook* (The Bible in American Culture, 5; Philadelphia: Fortress Press; Chico, CA: Scholars Press, 1982), and Ernest R. Sandeen (ed.), *The Bible and Social Reform* (The Bible in American Culture, 6; Philadelphia: Fortress Press; Chico, CA: Scholars Press, 1982).

biblical themes, given by Edwin Good as he strayed somewhat from his theme of 'The Bible and American Music'.[10]

It remains difficult to identify serious and systematic compilations of the presence of the Bible and biblical themes in culture, and I mention the only two such works known to me.

In the field of art, there is the unique three-volume work by Louis Réau, *Iconographie de l'art chrétien*,[11] of which the second and third volumes are devoted to the Old and New Testaments respectively. It is a *catalogue raisonnée*, arranged for the most part by biblical book order, and rich in references to individual works of art. Frequently Réau relates the iconography to contemporary literary interpretations. Jonah, for example, appears in Christian art almost exclusively as a symbol of resurrection and hardly ever as a prophet. He is a favourite in the art of the catacombs and on sarcophagi, but after the thirteenth century he almost disappears? Why? And why is he always *bald*? There is a PhD thesis topic here, one feels.

As for literature, there is really only one serious and comprehensive work I know of, and even it is restricted to literature in English: it is the recent encyclopaedia edited by David Lyle Jeffrey, *A Dictionary of Biblical Tradition in English Literature*.[12] With articles on biblical phrases, themes, images and characters and their reappearance or afterlife in literature, it offer us a massive testimonial to the presence of the Bible in our culture, the Bible in the modern world.

10. Edwin M. Good, 'The Bible and American Music', in Gunn (ed.), *The Bible and American Arts and Letters*, pp. 129-56 (152-53).

11. Louis Réau, *Iconographie de l'art chrétien*. Tome II. *Iconographie de la Bible*. I. *Ancien Testament* (Paris: Presses Universitaires de France, 1956). See also the helpful (and delightfully opinionated) general account by Pamela Tudor-Craig, 'Art, The Bible in', in *A Dictionary of Biblical Interpretation* (ed. R.J. Coggins and J.L. Houlden; London: SCM Press, 1990), pp. 57-65. There is also Marcel Brion and Heidi Heimann, *The Bible in Art: Miniatures, Paintings, Drawings and Sculptures Inspired by the Old Testament* (London: Phaidon, 1956); Jacob Leveen, *The Hebrew Bible in Art* (The Schweich Lectures, 1939; London: Oxford University Press, 1944).

12. David Lyle Jeffrey (ed.), *A Dictionary of Biblical Tradition in English Literature* (Grand Rapids: Eerdmans, 1992).

We could glance, for example, at biblical phrases that have become part of our speech: seven pillars of wisdom, the sheep and the goats, the scales fell from his eyes, the salt of the earth, sackcloth and ashes, shibboleth, signs of the times, sour grapes, spare the rod, a still small voice, the strait and narrow, suffer fools gladly, sufficient unto the day, swords into ploughshares—and this is just a selection of phrases with the initial letter 's'! Or we could note the titles of literary works that allude to the Bible:[13] Thomas Hobbes's *Leviathan*, Emily Dickinson's *Belshazzar Had a Letter*, Bernard Shaw's *Back to Methuselah*, Flanery O'Connor's *The Violent Bear It Away*, William Golding's *Lord of the Flies* (in reference to Beelzebub), and even including Eugene O'Neill's *The Iceman Cometh*, a reference to 'the bridegroom cometh' of the parable of the foolish virgins. Or we could find Sherlock Holmes speaking of a broken reed, the narrator in a P.G. Wodehouse novel murmuring 'Ichabod' to himself as he walks down Oxford Street,[14] Henderson the Rain King in Saul Bellow's novel re-enacting Nebuchadnezzar's transformation into a beast of the field, or T.S. Eliot's Nehemiah figure setting about his building of the new city, 'The trowel in hand, and the gun rather loose in the holster'.[15]

But Jeffreys's dictionary is not the only way into the gathering of the data. I have before me an excellent work by Sol Liptzin, *Biblical Themes in World Literature*,[16] with chapters on Defiant Cain, Rebekah's Beguilement of Isaac, Schiller's Moses, Elijah in Yiddish Literature, Job and Faust, and the like. Here too is *Biblical Patterns in Modern Literature*, edited by David H. Hirsch and Nehama Aschkenasy,[17] with essays on Chaucer and the Bible, biblical substructures in Hardy, the creation of Eve in Marcel Proust, and on and on. And there is Honor Matthews, *The Primal Curse: The Myth of Cain and Abel in the Theatre*,[18] in Middleton and

---

13. See, for example, Harold E. Holland, 'Fiction Titles from the Bible', *Oklahoma Librarian* 15 (1965), pp. 116-22; W. Kahoe, *Book Titles from the Bible* (Moylan, PA: The Rose Valley Press, 1946).

14. P.G. Wodehouse, *Ukridge* (London: Herbert Jenkins, 1924), p. 12.

15. *Choruses from 'The Rock'*, 5 (in T.S. Eliot, *Collected Poems 1909–1962* [London: Faber & Faber, 1974], p. 173).

16. Hoboken, NJ: Ktav, 1985.

17. Brown Judaic Studies, 77; Chico, CA: Scholars Press, 1984.

18. New York: Schocken Books, 1967.

Webster, Ibsen, Strindberg and Beckett. And here is *The Bible and the Narrative Tradition*, edited by Frank McConnell,[19] with essays by the literary gurus Harold Bloom, Hans Frei, Frank Kermode and Herbert Schneidau, announcing that the Bible is 'less a book and more a living entity in the evolving consciousness of Western man [*sic*]' and undertaking to explain how 'the Bible has achieved its permanent presence in, and influence upon, the whole of Western civilization'. And then there is Leslie Tannenbaum's *Biblical Tradition in Blake's Early Prophecies: The Great Code of Art*,[20] and Janet Larson's *Dickens and the Broken Scripture*,[21] and Harold Fisch's *Jerusalem and Albion: The Hebraic Factor in Seventeenth Century Literature*[22]—and dozens of others.[23] And they are just the books. It is a pretty impressive accounting, this trainspotting of biblical allusions and influences.[24] And most of it is a

19. New York: Oxford University Press, 1986.
20. Princeton: Princeton University Press, 1982.
21. Athens, GA: University of Georgia Press, 1985.
22. New York: Schocken Books, 1964.
23. Like Richmond Noble, *Shakespeare's Biblical Knowledge and Use of the Book of Common Prayer* (London: SPCK, 1935); Mary and Ellen Gibbs, *The Bible References of John Ruskin* (London: George Allen, 1898); David C. Fowler, *The Bible in Early English Literature* (London: Sheldon, 1977); Fowler, *The Bible in Middle English Literature* (Seattle: University of Washington Press, 1984); David Norton, *A History of the Bible as Literature* (2 vols.; Cambridge: Cambridge University Press, 1993); James Moffatt, *The Bible in Scots Literature* (London: Hodder & Stoughton, 1924); Duncan Anderson, *The Bible in Seventeenth-Century Scottish Life and Literature* (London: Allenson, 1936); David F. Wright, Ian Campbell and John Gibson (eds.), *The Bible in Scottish Life and Literature* (Edinburgh: St Andrew Press, 1988).
24. And not a word so far about the Bible and music, the Bible and drama (apart from Shakespeare), or the Bible and film. There are some references in *The Oxford Companion to Music* (ed. Percy A. Scholes; London: Oxford University Press, 10th edn ed. John Owen Ward, 1970), pp. 108, 276, 538, 837-38. See also Claude Abravanel and Betty Hirshowitz, *The Bible in English Music: W. Byrd—H. Purcell* (AMLI Studies in Music Bibliography, 1; Haifa: Haifa Music Museum and AMLI Library, 1970). And there is James Laster's *Catalogue of Choral Music Arranged in Biblical Order* (Metuchen: Scarecrow Press, 1983).
     On drama, see Murray Roston, *Biblical Drama in England: From the Middle Ages to the Present Day* (London: Faber & Faber, 1968); Roston, *Prophet and Poet: The Bible and the Growth of Romanticism* (London: Faber & Faber, 1965). I have found also Paul F. Casey, *The Susanna Theme in German Literature:*

fascinating read. But what does it all *mean*?

2. *Interpreting the Data about the Bible and Culture*

1. First, I want to know, Why are we interested in this question of the Bible's presence in culture? What need in ourselves does it address? What is our *will* in this matter,[25] and how might it improperly influence our judgment?

I think that it appeals to the biblical scholar and to religious believers who esteem the Bible to know that their text is also known in secular culture. When, in the 50s, I used to drive a VW Beetle on outback roads in Australia, I always waved to other drivers who had the good sense to be driving a VW too. The same club mentality holds good for sophisticated scholars and clean-living Bible believers. They wish it to be the case that people outside their relatively narrow circle should appreciate what they themselves are devoted to, and they get a frisson of delight in finding that eminent literary people are 'influenced', in whatever small measure, by a text that they themselves find all-important and all-significant. More, there is a will to power, a crusading, missionary zeal among aficionados of every stripe, that wills others to accept and esteem what they esteem.

I conclude from that analysis that biblical scholars and religious believers are unreliable witnesses when it comes to assessing the importance of the Bible in culture. They have too big an investment in the matter. That will explain why everything I have ever read on the subject seems to participate in a conspiracy of adulation of the Bible and its influence on culture.

Variations of the Biblical Drama (Abhandlungen zur Kunst-, Musik- und Literaturwissenschaft, 214; Bonn: Bouvier, 1976).

On film, see Larry J. Kreitzer, *The New Testament in Fiction and Film: On Reversing the Hermeneutical Flow* (The Biblical Seminar, 17; Sheffield: Sheffield Academic Press, 1993); Kreitzer, *The Old Testament in Fiction and Film: On Reversing the Hermeneutical Flow* (The Biblical Seminar, 24; Sheffield: Sheffield Academic Press, 1994).

25. It's a Nietzschean question (as in *The Will to Power* [trans. Walter Kaufmann and R.J. Hollingdale; London: Weidenfeld & Nicolson, 1968 (original edition, 1901)]). I hope that is not *bad*.

2. So my second question is: How influential *is* the Bible, really? I take down from the shelf *The Oxford Companion to the English Language*,[26] and look up 'Biblical English'. 'English literature', I read, 'is full of quotations in which Bible sentences or phrases are worked into an author's own language: Shakespeare, "come *the four corners of the world* in arms" (*King John*, c. 1595);... Kipling, a book title, *Thy Servant a Dog* (1930); Wodehouse: "I was one of the idle rich. I *toiled not, neither did I*—except for a bump supper at Cambridge—*spin*" (*Leave it to Psmith*, 1923)'.[27] '*Full of* biblical language, is it? How full is full? Compared to non-biblical language, how much biblical language is there in D.H. Lawrence, H.G. Wells, Iris Murdoch, Margaret Drabble, John Updike? I don't know, but I have the uncomfortable impression that someone is trying to *convince* me of something they feel strongly about, but which is not necessarily the case.

Or take this sentence, opening an article on English Poetry in Coggins's and Houlden's *A Dictionary of Biblical Interpretation*: 'It is almost universally acknowledged that the Bible is the most important single source of English literature'.[28] I can't help worrying about that 'almost'. How I would like to locate the deviants who *don't* acknowledge it, and learn their reasons! For if the 'acknowledgment' is not universal, it isn't fact, is it, but only an opinion—and so it's debatable. And I wonder too about the 'most important single source', since it doesn't rule out there being many and much more important other sources that happen to be more complex—especially when the writer goes on to allow that 'until the nineteenth century classical culture...furnished English poets with as much material for their verse as the Bible'. The fact that 'there was no single source from which this [classical] material was chosen, so that the exact location of a classical story or allusion is often difficult to trace' does not imply that their influence is less than that of the Bible, as the writer seems to suggest. Rhetoric aside, how important *is* the Bible in literature?

26. Ed. Tom McArthur; Oxford: Oxford University Press, 1992.

27. P.G. Wodehouse, *Leave It to Psmith* (London: Barrie & Jenkins, 1924), pp. 123-25 (124).

28. Brian Horne, 'Poetry, English', in *A Dictionary of Biblical Interpretation* (ed. R.J. Coggins and J.L. Houlden; London: SCM Press, 1990), pp. 549-53 (549).

Is there any way of *quantifying* the place of the Bible in culture? I had an idea. Think of a medium, I said to myself, through which the culture of Western civilization reaches us, and which you can *quantify*. Quick as a shot the answer came: the Third Programme of the BBC as it was, BBC Radio Three.[29] So I thought, Let's see where and how the Bible is represented on this smorgasbord of culture.

My chosen week began on March 27, a Saturday, you might happen to remember. There are not, incidentally, many calendrical systems in which the week begins on a Saturday, certainly not in the Jewish-Christian tradition. But in the world of the *Radio Times*, that typically British institution in which the name is traditional but largely untrue (not one page in eight is allocated to the times of radio programmes), the week begins on Saturday.

To get to the point: Among the offerings on Radio Three, where was the Bible? On Saturday, there was no Bible, unless some snippets from Bach's Motets in Record Review were biblical. I missed it. On Sunday, a few minutes by Anon gave us *Surrexit de Tumulo* and an *Agnus Dei*, Walton's *Facade* played intertextual mischief with biblical language, and the evening heard a full *St John Passion* from the modern Estonian composer Arvo Pärt (85 minutes). On Monday Elisabeth Söderstrom sang two pieces by Rachmaninov, *O Mother of God* and *Perpetually Praying* (which may have been biblical, but they were in Russian, so I can't tell you for sure). On Tuesday there were *Three Sacred Choruses* by Brahms (15 minutes) and a programme of fifteenth-century church music, probably biblical in the main (35 minutes). On Wednesday Elisabeth Söderstrom was still singing, this time Rachmaninov's *Christ is Risen* and the *Lord's Prayer* from the Liturgy of St John Chrysostom; and we had the opening section of the *Passione di Gesù Cristo* by Paisiello and two sonatas from Haydn's *Seven Last Words of our Saviour on the Cross*, and Choral Evensong from Southwell Minster with Psalms 147–50 and readings from the RSV of Jeremiah 33 and John 13. On Thursday we heard Bach's cantata *Widerstehe doch der Sünde*, a second programme of fifteenth-century church music, and an oratorio

29. It broadcasts mostly classical music and drama, the very bellwether of high culture among the media in Britain.

by one Johann Joseph Fux, *La Deposizione della Croce*, commem-
orating the taking down of Christ from the cross, and first per-
formed in Vienna in 1728. On Friday there was choral music by
Rachmaninov, *Blessed Art Thou O Lord*, from his *Vespers*.

But that was the week before Easter. Perhaps it was not very
typical. This week we had, on Saturday, Elgar's oratorio *The
Kingdom* (30 minutes), Bernstein's *Mass*, and Milhaud's *La création
du monde*. On Sunday, there was Handel's Coronation Anthem
My Heart is Inditing, with the words of Psalm 45, and Bliss's Suite
Things to Come, of which the title at least is biblical, and there
was Mozart's *Mass in C minor*. On Monday, Handel being composer of the week, there was an hour of Handel's *Saul* ('To be
sure, it will be most excessive noisy', Lord Wentworth predicted
in 1739), Prokofiev's *Overture on Hebrew Themes*, *Three Psalms* by
Honegger, a setting of Heine's poem on the death of Belshazzar
by Berthold Goldschmidt to symbolize the defeat of Nazism,
under the Radio Times (biblical) headline of The Writing on the
Wall, and some organ music from Messiaen's *Messe de la Pen-
tecôte*. On Tuesday an hour from Handel's *Belshazzar*, 'the most
striking lesson against common genteel swearing I ever met with'
according to Miss Carter of 1745. For Wednesday, there is an hour
from Handel's *Solomon*, 'a noble piece, very grand and uncom-
mon', according to Mr Handel himself, and Choral Evensong
from Salisbury, with readings from Job and Acts and settings of
several psalms. Thursday the Handel is from *Susanna* ('I believe
it will insinuate itself into my approbation', said Lady Shaftes-
bury [1749]), and Mozart's aria *Exsultate, jubilate*. Friday, no Bible
on Radio Three.

And what does all that *mean*?

1. No one is sitting in Broadcasting House, monitoring the
amount of exposure the Bible is getting, I presume. This is the
culture unselfconscious of itself.

2. The Bible is certainly there, most days.

3. It is not privileged, not even signalled as being the Bible. It is
not revered, but neither is it treated as anything odd. It does not
defile the hands.

4. It is there for Handel's sake, not for its own. William Cowper,
the poet and hymnwriter (1731–1800), would not have been
amused:

> Ten thousand sit
> Patiently present at a sacred song,
> Commemoration-mad; content to hear
> (Oh wonderful effect of music's pow'r!)
> Messiah's eulogy for Handel's sake![30]

5. It is not going out of fashion, if the twentieth-century names, Prokofiev, Rachmaninov, Messiaen, Milhaud, Bernstein, Honegger, Berthold Goldschmidt and Arvo Pärt are anything to go by.

6. There was no *speech* about the Bible on Radio Three—except for lessons from the Bible within broadcast church services—but only musical settings of words from the Bible, or works inspired by some biblical idea or narrative.

7. It is a fraction of the culture. Radio Three is on the air 120 hours a week, and the Bible gets five or six hours, 5% or so. Is this a lot or a little? Perhaps these were both exceptional weeks, with Easter and with Handel being composer of the week.[31] Even so, the Bible has its percentage. But how are we to assess that percentage? Shall we say, The Bible is compulsory? Or shall we say, The Bible is marginal? Could we say, for example, that the Bible could be eliminated from the musical culture and we wouldn't notice the difference (except of course from missing some of our favourite works)? I heard the other day of a composer from Bulgaria who had never heard any church music all his professional career and had to catch up with everything on his arrival in Britain last year. What exactly was he missing?

3. My third question is, Where in the culture is the Bible most at home? Can we locate foci of its influence? My answers here are more impressionistic still, but my guess is that we have just now been looking at the most biblically saturated element of our culture: music.

What of art? Perhaps if we looked at the whole historical sweep of fine art, at the range of paintings accessible in our museums,

---

30. *The Task*, 6.633-37 (in *The Poetical Works of William Cowper* [ed. H.S. Milford; London: Oxford University Press, 4th edn, 1934], p. 233).

31. I kept on analysing the Radio Times. For the week beginning May 1, 1993, the only biblical presence was the Bach cantata, *Herr, gehe nicht ins Gericht*, Choral Evensong, and, if you can count them, Poulenc's *Gloria* and Bruckner's *Ave Maria*—which is to say, not more than two hours in all.

we might find a similar amount of representation of the Bible. But my feeling is that you would go a long way to find biblical themes in twentieth-century art, except of course art specifically commissioned for ecclesiastical settings. There was Rembrandt and Georges de la Tour, there was Blake and the Pre-Raphaelites, but '[w]hat has happened since?', asks Pamela Tudor-Craig in her article on the Bible in art for the *Dictionary of Biblical Interpretation*. She can mention Stanley Spencer's astonishing Resurrection in Cookham Churchyard, Graham Sutherland's 'rejected barbed-wire crucifix for Ely cathedral, and his *Noli me tangere* (camp follower's version!) at Chichester, as we have his Christ in Majesty at Coventry'.[32] But the abstract art of this century has obviously not found the Bible congenial. All the same, with the new realism of our own times, Pamela Tudor-Craig asks, could not our generation, 'which at the last moment has laboriously discovered the unity of this fragile creation, re-enter the Gardens of Eden and of the resurrection?'[33]

What then of our poets? The Bible is embedded in our Milton and our Shakespeare, in our Donne and our Herbert, of course, so it will never go off the curriculum. But what of the moderns, our Wallace Stevens, Theodore Roethke, Adrienne Rich,, Edwin Muir, Ted Hughes, Douglas Dunn, Seamus Heaney, Sylvia Plath, Peter Redgrove? It's a mixed bag.[34] I read through again Douglas Dunn's *Elegies*, wonderfully moving and evocative poems after the death of his wife, and there wasn't a biblical phrase or image in the whole volume. And then I opened the *Faber Book of Modern Verse*, and came across *Intimate Supper* by Peter Redgrove:

> He switched on the electric light and laughed,
> He let light shine in the firmament of his ceiling,
> He saw the great light shine around and it was good…
> He spun the great winds through his new hoover

32. Ed. R.J. Coggins and J.L. Houlden; London: SCM Press, 1990, pp. 57-65.

33. Tudor-Craig, 'Art, The Bible in', *Dictionary of Biblical Interpretation*, p. 65.

34. And I notice that in the article 'Poetry, English', by Brian Horne, in *A Dictionary of Biblical Interpretation* (ed. R.J. Coggins and J.L. Houlden; London: SCM Press, 1990), pp. 549-53, the last poet included is T.S. Eliot.

And let light be in the kitchen and that was good too...
And skipped to the bathroom and spun the shining taps
Dividing air from the deep, and the water, good creature,
Gave clouds to his firmament for he had raked the bowels
Of the seamy coal that came from the deep earth.
And he created him Leviathan and wallowed there,
Rose, and made his own image in the steamy mirrors...
But the good sight faded
For there was no help, no help meet for him at all,
And he set his table with two stars pointed on wax...
And until the time came that he had appointed
Walked in his garden in the cool of the evening, waited.[35]

Whatever you say about it, you have to call that biblical, even though its author is no Christian. I can only infer that the Bible is a *resource* for poets; they can take it or leave it. The naturalism and pointillism of much modern poetry does not accommodate the Bible, does not resonate with it. But the Bible's images and language still have a great capacity for intriguing and stimulating poets.

4. My fourth question is: What happens to the Bible when it is used in the context of general culture? And is such use good for the Bible or not?

There are two main characteristics of the use of the Bible in culture that I can identify. The first is that it is used piecemeal, the second that it is always altered when it is used, the third is that it is rarely acknowledged. These three facts make the use of the Bible problematic, obviously.

a. It is inherent in the idea of a source or influence that it will be drawn on only from time to time; and it will not reappear in a new literary work in its original form. Otherwise there would be no new literary work. We have identified in our data collection how in fact the Bible *is* used in literature, by piecemeal quotation of phrases out of context, by the adoption of images from the text, and so on. Now if the Bible had been a random collection of aphorisms, like the book of Proverbs, such use would not have been problematic. But so much of the Bible consists of unified narratives, poems and discourses that we have to wonder whether

35. *The Faber Book of Modern Verse* (ed. Michael Roberts; fourth edition revised by Peter Porter; London: Faber & Faber, 1982), p. 399.

such treatment constitutes 'use', and especially whether it is 'fair use'. There certainly isn't a lot of attempt in the cultural use of the Bible to *understand* the biblical text, especially the larger units of the biblical text; it is 'use' in the most pragmatic sense, 'use' almost in the sense of 'plunder'. It is interesting to compare how we 'use' other texts: these days, writers usually cite whole sentences and try to respect what they take to be the overall meaning of the whole work from which they are quoting. But you don't find a lot of verse references to the Bible in literature.

   b. All re-use of a text constitutes adaptation of it, even if only through the process of selection; and the use of the Bible piecemeal increases the amount of alteration involved. But the degree of alteration of the Bible in literature is more marked than that: it almost seems characteristic of the re-use of the Bible that its sense is deliberately altered. We saw a comic transformation of the text in the Wodehouse sentence about the idle who toil not neither do they 'spin'; we noticed in the Autumn Gold advertisement three points at which the Adam and Eve story had been altered by the tradition. The Peter Redgrove poem changed the text of Genesis by conflating the figures of God and Adam: it is of course God who creates the light and walks in the garden, but Adam for whom no help is found. Another, almost classical, example of wilful alteration is in the poem by Wilfred Owen, *The Parable of the Old Man and the Young*, which begins as a telling of the Genesis 22 story of Abraham's near-sacrifice of Isaac, but ends with the old man rejecting the angel's advice:

> But the old man would not so, but slew his son,
> And half the seed of Europe, one by one.[36]

   c. The third characteristic of the use of the Bible in literature is that it is typically not acknowledged. There is a complicity between author and reader here, an unspoken agreement that both know that it is the Bible that is being quoted, and that there is a deliberate adaptation of it. P.G. Wodehouse does not hint that he is quoting the Bible, and a non-Bible reader would be at a loss to see what was funny about his sentence. The closure of Wilfred Owen's poem is effective because he can trust his readership to

   36. Wilfred Owen, in C. Day Lewis (ed.), *The Collected Poems of Wilfred Owen* (London: Chatto & Windus, 1963), p. 42.

know the biblical text he is playing off against. It is the very opposite of the scrupulous acknowledgment of sources writers usually feel bound to go in for these days.

The question then is, Is this kind of use good for the Bible? On the ground that all publicity is good publicity, I'm inclined to say yes. Assuming that we are talking about image and recognition here, it is surely in the interest of the Bible—I mean, what the Bible stands for, whatever that is—that it gets referred to, even if it is unacknowledged or altered or 'distorted'.

In the first place, I shouldn't worry about it not getting credits ('Novel title and smart, pithy quotations from the Bible, with special thanks to St Paul and the anonymous author of Genesis'); I always think it's much better to get your ideas accepted than to have them acknowledged. So long as your idea bears your name, it's one idea among others and infinitely open to objection; but ideas without father or mother are literally common sense: no one says, Lunch on May 6; is that according to the Gregorian calendar? And think of the difference between 'Einstein's theory of relativity' and 'the theory of relativity'.

And as for 'distortions' of the Bible, there are two points to be made. One is that much of the use of the Bible actually depends on an agreed understanding of the text; thus the force of Wilfred Owen's poem derives from the fixity and known flow of the biblical text, and Wodehouse's wordplay would not work except as a self-conscious play with the undistorted biblical text. Peter Redgrove's conflation of God and Adam is a misrepresentation of the text, by most people's standards; but it deceives no one. It is a playful reworking that invites us to imagine the lonely gardener as the creator-as-householder—and vice versa.

This brings us near to the second point: Talk of distortion only makes sense if you begin from the idea of a fixed text with a determinate meaning that can be exegeted. Sometimes that's not a bad model to have in mind, and students of the Bible should certainly be trained to exegete texts, saying as precisely as possible what their wording allows, implies, negates, and the like. But that is not the only meaning of 'meaning'—as we all recognize when we say things like, 'I'm not sure what you mean by that', where we locate meaning somewhere other than in the words themselves. And if, to put it more theoretically, meaning is not some inherent property of texts, but what happens to readers reading, it doesn't make sense to talk of meanings being 'right' or 'wrong'—not in themselves, that is. Everything depends on the context, and what those who control the context determine is appropriate for it. I wouldn't allow Wodehouse's interpretation of 'spin' in an exegesis paper on the Gospels (I am in control, you need to know, on behalf of the academic guild, of what students can and cannot write in examination papers), but if I were to have been a reviewer of his novel I couldn't have faulted it. Maybe we don't approve of the context—someone might disapprove, for example, of making comic use of words in the Gospels—and so we would disapprove of all the meanings created within that context. But it would not be a matter of rejecting the meaning or interpretation or use because it did not conform to the rules of another context.

Distortion, in any case, might be a creative and positive form of interpretation. A caricature of a celebrity might reveal a truth about their appearance that a photograph never could, and a satire through its very exaggeration might be a more powerful exegetical tool than any painstaking commentary. Think of Swift's *Modest Proposal for Preventing the Children of Poor People in Ireland from Being a Burden to their Parents* (by fattening them up and selling them to the rich for food). Let us revert to the case of Peter Redgrove's poem. Is it not inviting us, by its confusion of the distinction between God and Adam, to reconsider the relationship between creator and creature. Is the utter disjunction between the two that Christian theology insists on necessarily appropriate?, we find ourselves asking. Poets as creators do not draw such sharp demarcations between themselves and their creations, and all of us know what it is like to put a lot of ourselves into our work. So when we are confronted with the character in *Intimate Supper* who lets light shine in the firmament of his ceiling and makes his own image in the bathroom mirror, but then starts to feel miserable because there is 'no help meet for him at all', might we not fall to thinking: Adam is, after all, walking around with God's breath in him; he is the image of God, and made in the likeness of God. So while it is literally an error that the 'he' in the poem should be both God and Adam, this deliberate distortion of the familiar text engenders interesting and perhaps novel ideas, so that we murmur *felix culpa* to the poet and go on reading him. Not only so, but we may turn to the text again and read it backwards, viewing the picture of the deity of Genesis 1 in the light of his creation, Adam, in Genesis 2. It is not good for the man to be alone—we have the divine word for it. Was it good then for the god to be alone? If the creature needs a 'helper', what of the creature's creator? 'One is one and all alone, and evermore shall be so'; is that any kind of life for a deity? And, come to think of it, how does God know that 'it is not good for the man to be alone'? Is he perhaps speaking from personal experience? What, we wonder, must the loneliness of a monotheistic deity be like? And what must the strains and stresses be for a divine single parent?

Of course, you may well say No! to such a line of thought. Just because it is novel and creative we are not compelled to believe it has any other merit. All the same, goodness knows, we do need creative interpretations of the Bible—and I know you will always call interpretations of mine you do not agree with 'distortions'!

5. The fifth question for this lecture is: Is the Bible, in the way it is used, good for the culture or not?

The first thing we need to recognize is that the Bible has no authoritative status in the culture, and so it is not allowed to say anything that the culture does not want said. That may be a bit depressing to believers in the Bible, who both grant the Bible a distinctive authority and who regard it as a norm that stands outside the culture. But if the culture as a whole took that view, it would itself be Christian—a situation that might not even be wholly desirable but is in any case clearly not the situation we find ourselves in.

But the other side to this point is that our modern culture (I am still speaking of 'high' culture) is very diverse, very pluralist, and very open—compared at any rate with that of contemporary China or sixteenth-century Geneva. So there is a good chance that the Bible will in one way or another, in one context or another, have its voice heard in our culture. And the culture is in the main very supportive of the Bible and appreciative of its qualities. People do not refer to the Bible in order to attack it. No one says that it is bad literature, that it lowers the moral tone of the culture, that it should be phased out of our schools like Biggles or Enid Blyton. It is often ignored, but the culture is not in standing conflict with it.

Even when the biblical text is altered, denatured or distorted, there is not necessarily any criticism of the Bible itself. Take again the case of Wilfred Owen's poem. When the Aqedah story is re-run in the modern world, his poem is saying, it does not have the happy ending it has in the Bible. The contemporary Isaac is not rescued at the last moment; the seed of Europe, half of it, at any rate, is slain, one by one. For Owen, indeed, the biblical narrative is the norm, against which the modern world is weighed and found wanting. Now I wouldn't be surprised if there is not also a certain bitterness here against the Bible, an implicit protest that the Bible led us to expect a happier issue from danger than reality allows, that the Bible has a fairytale quality. But any complaint against the Bible is marginal compared with the poet's rage against the futility and horror of modern warfare.

So what we find is that the culture does not accord the Bible any truly authoritative status, and yet it is quite respectful of it and sympathetic to it. Our culture expresses any discomfort it feels with the Bible mainly by ignoring it. Is all this to the benefit of the culture?

On the positive side, the Bible is obviously still an important source of inspiration for imaginative writing. Its images and its narratives still resonate with the issues of our time. The notion of creativity, for example, that gives us personal authorization when we sit down to write an essay or set about decorating a new

---

37. Biggles is a fictional flying ace of the First World War in boys' books by Captain W.E. Johns, not the kind of thing we want future citizens of the European Union or embryonic new men to be brought up on (some sample titles are: *Biggles Flies West* [London: Oxford University Press, 1937], *Biggles Defies the Swastika* [London: Oxford University Press, 1942], *Biggles Sweeps the Desert* [London: Hodder & Stoughton, 1941]). Enid Blyton's stories of life in boarding schools were hugely popular with children who never went to one, and were probably the founding myth of those who did, but their ethnocentricity makes them unsuitable in a multicultural society (some sample titles: *In the Fifth at Malory Towers* [London: Methuen, 1950], *The Twins at St Clare's* [London: Methuen, 1941], *The Naughtiest Girl in the School* [London: Newnes, 1940]).

house, bears the influence of Genesis 1 with its story of purpose, design and effectual execution. We are not ourselves the Creator, but our own creativity—even our very concept of creativity—is somehow shaped by the idea of the possibility of creation and the expression of that possibility in the biblical writing. The horror stories of the Bible, of the universal flood or the genocide of the Canaanites or the rape of Tamar or the death of the innocents, put into words anxieties that lie for the most part at the unconscious level but that need to be addressed from time to time. Their realization and expression in these ancient mythic texts enable us to face anxieties of our own that are too close for comfort, to get the measure of them, to objectify and distance them, and to recognize that they are not ours alone, but the common burden of the human race. Or, take a different example, the longings that come to expression in the Bible, whether they take the shape of the longing for Jerusalem ('If I forget thee, let my right hand forget its cunning') or for the divine ('As the hart pants after the waterbrooks, so pants my soul after you, O God') or for the Other ('Let him kiss me with the kisses of his mouth, for your love is better than wine'). Culture needs to have images of this intensity, to remind itself of the potency of dreams precisely in a technological age, and to awaken desire within humans in the midst of everyday and deadening routines.

But there is a downside too to the use of the Bible in culture. I identify four elements:

a. The Bible that we encounter in our culture is a fragmented Bible. I am not at this point worried about whether that is fair or unfair to the Bible, whether it does the Bible itself any harm, but whether it is bad for the culture. I think it is, because the culture is under a misapprehension. It thinks it knows the Bible, but it knows the Bible mainly as a book of quotes. It knows its purple passages and its most dramatic moments. But it does not know its longueurs; it does not know its rhythms and its shape. It does not know it as a whole, and therefore it does not know its variety, for its variety is only a function of its unity.

b. Culture attributes authority to its classics. So while the Bible has no authority of its own in the culture, and is not allowed to say anything the culture does not want to hear, when its voice does coincide with the culture's, the culture thinks it has the

Bible on its side. This is why all kinds of unlikely people, including the devil, quote Scripture—to their own advantage. But it is a spurious authority, any authority that comes into play only when I choose it shall. And I think it is bad for the morals of the society to think that they can have Scripture's backing when it suits them—and not buy the whole package.

c. What culture commonly (though not always) siphons off from the Bible is the element of the divine. The Bible is, of course, a human book. However firmly you believe in the divine inspiration of the Bible, you had better believe just as firmly in the human inspiration of the Bible, otherwise you may get a reputation as a docetist. It is a book that addresses fundamental human concerns, and every page in it was written, authored, composed, by a human being—just as much as Jesus was in every respect a thoroughly human being. But it wouldn't be the book it is if its central concern was not the divine. And secular culture has some trouble handling that central concern. Wherever the culture is unable to make a space for religious belief, for the legitimacy of God-talk, for the psychological normalcy of humans who believe in the supernatural, at that point the culture is harming itself by pretending it knows the Bible. And when it thinks it can have the Bible stripped of the divine, it is kidding itself. 'Those who talk of the Bible as "a monument of English prose" are merely admiring it as a monument over the grave of Christianity', said T.S. Eliot.[38]

d. Finally, it does the culture harm when its way of disagreeing with the Bible is to ignore it. The very respectfulness of the culture toward the Bible, its tacit decision to accentuate the positive, is an abdication of responsibility. The culture would do itself a favour to enter into dialogue with the Bible, and to sort out why it wants to plunder the Bible for its images and its language while refusing to accept it as *truth*. If that means more criticism of the Bible than we are used to in the Sunday papers, more satire, more unreasonable attacks on biblical values, so be it. The Bible needs all the publicity it can get.

38. T.S. Eliot, 'Religion and Literature' (1935), in his *Selected Essays* (London: Faber & Faber, 1951), pp. 388-401.

Chapter 3

THE BIBLE AND THE PUBLIC

Who owns the Bible? In this country, almost everyone. Who is
entitled to read the Bible? Everyone. Who actually does read the
Bible? Half the population. Who has opinions about the Bible?
Absolutely everyone.

That means to say, the Bible is a book belonging to the public,
to the society at large. It is not the preserve of the academy, of
the church, or of the high culture of the society. Not to say that
the boy that driveth the plough doth whistle it at his work, as
Tyndale hoped.

Many people who have no axe to grind, religious or academic,
think the Bible is the most important book in the world, the most
influential work in English literature. And the Bible still outsells
every other book.[1] It is a very public text.

So it is very surprising that no one seems to be very interested
in the public of Bible buyers and Bible readers. I can find no studies at all of what people in this country think about the Bible, how
they understand it, what they think of its truth or otherwise, if
and how they use it.

You might have thought that some academic somewhere might
have researched it, or that churches that thought evangelism was
more than dumping unwanted tracts onto people might have
commissioned surveys into what their targeted audiences

---

1.   What that fact means is of course open to question. Daniel Boorstin
wrote: 'In the twentieth century our highest praise is to call the Bible "The
World's Best Seller". And it has come to be more and more difficult to say
whether we think it is a best seller because it is great, or vice versa' (Daniel
J. Boorstin, *The Image: What Happened to the American Dream* [London:
Weidenfeld & Nicolson, 1961], p. 122; also published as *The Image: A Guide
to Pseudo-Events in America* [New York: Atheneum, 1971])

already knew and believed about the Bible. Well, if anyone has done any such thing, they have kept it well hidden. I have given up my searches. Even the Bible Societies, which exist for no other purposes than promoting the Bible and don't have the upkeep of redundant cathedrals to worry about, don't seem to have considered the matter. They have done a couple of surveys of people's Bible-buying habits, and of churchgoers' Bible-reading habits. But they have never studied the public's knowledge or use of the Bible or opinions about it.

There was only one way to find out what I wanted to find out. I had to do it myself. Fortunately I had the services of my class of 50 students for The Bible in the Modern World. Perhaps I should tell you something about this course, known in the department as BMW—an acronym that has, I trust, the right flavour of style, luxury and flair.

Here is how I presented it to my students, in my module description in 1992:

> The idea behind The Bible in the Modern World is that most of our courses are essentially about the Bible as an ancient text but the Bible itself is not just an ancient text. It also exists, as we do, in the modern world; so one way of studying it would be to find out what happens to the Bible in our own culture, and what it does to people today if they read it.
>
> Unlike the 'ancient' questions about the Bible (who wrote it? why? when? inasmuch as which?), where there are more than enough textbooks to keep you going for a lifetime, there are no textbooks (to speak of) about the Bible in the modern world. Try James Barr's *The Bible in the Modern World*,[2] for example, or Dennis Nineham's *The Use and Abuse of the Bible*,[3] and you'll see what I mean.
>
> So this course moves in uncharted territory. You will not get good lecture notes, it will be frustrating and demanding and you won't always know where you (or the course) are going. But you will be *in charge of your own learning*, and not just following someone else's programme.

2.   James Barr, *The Bible in the Modern World* (London: SCM Press, 1973).
3.   Dennis Nineham, *The Use and Abuse of the Bible: A Study of the Bible in an Age of Rapid Cultural Change* (Library of Philosophy and Religion; London: Macmillan, 1976).

We'll do this course as a kind of project, in which we'll coop-
erate (not compete for 'marks'), and in which we'll work collectively, in small groups (of three). I would like us to have two aims:
1. to *find out* how the Bible is actually being used in the modern
world (Term 1); 2. to *evaluate* the uses to which the Bible is put
(Term 2).

Last time (two years ago), the class decided to do three surveys
of how the Bible is being used: in churches (and the synagogue),
in schools, and as general knowledge among the public. They wrote
group reports on the first two areas, and for the third they carried
out a street survey with a questionnaire they designed. In the second term, we looked at the views of the Bible on two ethical questions, war and sex, and at the ways the biblical statements are being
used in the modern world.

This year's class can decide to do things differently, as long as it
is addressing the course aims. You could, for example, be a bit more
highbrow and ask how the Bible affects contemporary culture. Or
you could be a bit more lowbrow and find out how the Bible is
perceived and used in the popular press. And in the second term
we could get more involved with scholarly and popular literature
about the Bible and ethical questions than we did before.

The aim of the course is to give you experience in working as a
member of a group, in participating in the design of a project, in
time management, in interviewing skills, in oral presentational
skills. It also inevitably raises questions about what biblical studies is, about the relation of the scholarly tradition to lived experience, about the distinction between academic and non-academic—
and about what education is all for and about anyway.

That was the context from which this course of lectures arose.
And in this lecture I want to present two elements of the class's
work. The first is the results of their street survey; the second is
the collection of materials from the daily press. In the next lecture, on the Bible and the church, I shall draw upon the class's
visits to Sheffield churches and synagogues. In both lectures, I
want to move all the time beyond mere data to interpretation, and
make generalizations that are interesting or at least provocative.
But I do put a lot of store by the data, not because they are very
exhaustive or scientifically gathered, but because they are data
that have perhaps not previously been collected and so have
some degree of originality about them.

I have to admit that the size of the sample was not very large, that our sample was chosen randomly, and that the questionnaires left a lot of room open for improvement. But on the other hand, I should remark that the number of interviewees in a normal national opinion poll is often not much more than 1000, and that I believe that if a thing is worth doing, it's worth doing badly—if you don't have the time or skill to do it well—and also, to any disposed to be critical, that I prefer our way of doing it to your way of not doing it! In general, I am prepared to argue that the results of our Sheffield survey are likely to be true enough for the country generally (I mean England, since Scotland and Northern Ireland are very different religiously) for some meaningful conclusions to be drawn.

1. *Sheffield Street Survey: The Bible and the Public, 1990 and 1992*

Perhaps it would be best for you to see first the questionnaires we designed. Since the format of the questionnaires was a class project, they were designed afresh by each class, though the class of 1992 saw the 1990 questionnaire when they had drafted theirs, and incorporated a number of ideas from the earlier questionnaire.

a. *The 1990 Questionnaire*

THE BIBLE IN THE MODERN WORLD

Street Survey, 1990

Excuse me. I wonder if you would like to help me with a survey I'm doing. I'm a student at the University, and we're doing a survey about the Bible. That's my subject. It'll just take a few minutes. Thank you.

We've got a few questions about stories from the Bible.

1. Do you remember the name of Jesus' mother? Was it
    a. Elizabeth?
    b. Mary?
    c. Martha?
2. How long ago, roughly, would you say Jesus was born?
3. At the beginning of the Bible, Adam and Eve were the first humans. Did they live
    a. in a cave?
    b. in a garden?
    c. on a hill?

---

4. Noah was famous for
     a. the ten commandments
     b. being swallowed by a whale
     c. building a boat
5. How many Gospels are there in the Bible?
     a. two
     b. four
     c. twelve
6. Would you like to tell me which of these ideas about the Bible you agree with?
     a. The Bible is full of myths and legends.
     b. The Bible is true.
     c. The Bible is too religious for me.
     d. The Bible is really just ancient history.
     e. The Bible is a great comfort when you're in trouble.
7. When would you say you last actually read any of the Bible?
8. When would you say you were last in a church?
9. Do you have a Bible of your own?
10. Would you mind telling me what is your job?

That's all I need to ask you, thanks very much. We're doing a course on how people in Sheffield think about the Bible, and there are 35 of us out here doing interviews. Thank you very much for helping me.

[When the interviewee has left, note down M/F and your estimate of age (20s, 50s, etc.)]

b. *The 1992 Questionnaire*

Interviewee number.....

Male/Female?....

THE BIBLE IN THE MODERN WORLD

Street Survey, 1992

Excuse me. I wonder if you would like to help me with a survey I'm doing. I'm a student at the University, and we're doing a survey about the Bible. That's my subject. It'll just take a few minutes. Thank you.

We've got a few questions about stories from the Bible.

1. At the beginning of the Bible, Adam and Eve were the first humans. Did they live
     a. in a cave?
     b. in a garden?
     c. on a hill?

2. Do you remember why Noah built the ark? Was it
    a. to keep the ten commandments in?
    b. because it was going to rain?
    c. so as to hide from God?
3. Who had a donkey who talked? Was it
    a. Balaam?
    b. Jesus?
    c. Moses?
4. Jesus told a story about the Good Samaritan. He helped a man who was
    a. ill
    b. robbed
    c. suicidal
5. When Jesus fed 5000 hungry people, he gave them
    a. bread and cheese
    b. bread and figs
    c. bread and fish
6. Where did Jesus die? In
    a. Jerusalem?
    b. Bethlehem?
7. Do you have a Bible of your own?
8. When would you say you last read any of the Bible?
9. Do you think children should be taught the Bible?
10. Do you think they should be taught in school?
11. Were you taught the Bible in school?
12. Would you like to tell me which of these ideas about the Bible you agree with?
    a. The Bible is full of myths and legends
    b. The Bible is true.
    c. The Bible is too religious for me.
    d. The Bible is really just ancient history.
    e. The Bible is good for telling you what's right and wrong.
    f. The Bible is a great comfort when you're in trouble.
13. When would you say you were last in church?
14. Would you mind telling me what is your job?
15. And could you tell me, please, are you in your twenties/thirties...?
[or whatever seems appropriate]

That's all I need to ask you, thanks very much. We're doing a course on how people in Sheffield think about the Bible, and there are 50 of us out here doing interviews. Thank you very much for helping me.

c. *Notes on the Questionnaires*

1. As you will see, in both questionnaires we distinguished questions about Bible knowledge from evaluative questions.

2. By noting people's sex, and asking about their age and occupation, we hoped to distinguish between differences within our samples.

3. The 1990 survey interviewed 144 people, the 1992 survey 245. Both surveys were carried out mainly on The Moor in Sheffield, a pedestrianized shopping street containing British Home Stores, Marks and Spencer, and Debenhams,[4] but not specialty stores or boutiques. Readers can draw their own conclusions about the likely classes of the population that shop in that street. The survey was carried out in the December of each year.

4. Both questionnaires were pre-tested by each interviewer on a friend for intelligibility and difficulty.

d. *Results of the 1990 Questionnaire*

	Bible Knowledge and Evaluation, 1992				
	% correct	*a*	*b*	*c*	
1. Jesus' mother	99.3	0.7	99.3	0.0	
2. 2000 yrs ago	75.7	75.7	13.9	10.4	[a: right, b: wrong; c: don't know]
3. Adam & Eve	95.1	4.2	95.1	0.7	
4. Noah	89.6	4.9	5.6	89.6	
5. Gospels	64.3	64.3	4.2	31.0	[a: right, b: wrong; c: don't know]
6. Bible is . . .					
a. myth?	41.7				
b. true?	43.1				
c. too religious?	22.9				
d. ancient history?	27.1				
e. comfort?	42.4				
7. Last read?					
a. last week	18.6				
b. last month	8.3				
c. last year	18.6				
d. long ago	50.0				
e. never	5.5				
8. Last in church?					
a. last week	27.6				
b. last month	15.9				
c. last year	36.6				
d. long ago	17.9				
e. never	2.1				
9. Own Bible	78.3		18.6	3.1	[a: yes, b: no, c: don't know]

4.   Three well-known chains of department stores in Britain.

e. *Results of the 1992 Questionnaire*

	Bible Knowledge, 1992, by Sex and Age									
	% correct	M	F	-20	20s	30s	40s	50s	60s	70+
1. Adam and Eve	89.5	94	92	94	96	94	90	85	100	93
2. Noah	85.9	85	87	94	91	84	80	76	82	93
3. Balaam	64.2	63	61	65	62	58	65	64	55	71
4. Samaritan	78.8	77	77	76	76	74	88	76	64	86
5. 5000	92.7	91	93	94	94	90	98	82	100	93
6. Jerusalem	67.2	61	71	59	72	70	72	61	45	43
No. of respondents	244	124	121	17	79	50	40	33	11	14
avge % correct	88	78	80	80	82	78	82	74	74	80

	Bible Evaluation, 1992, by Sex and Age									
	% yes	M	F	-20	20s	30s	40s	50s	60s	70+
7. own Bible?	71.8	61	81	65	68	68	72	73	82	93
8. last read?										
a. last week	22.6	18	26	12	20	12	35	30	18	29
b. last month	9.7	10	10	12	11	14	8	9	0	0
c. last year	13.7	15	13	24	16	14	12	6	9	14
d. long ago	46.0	49	43	35	51	48	42	36	55	50
e. never	8.1	9	7	18	3	12	2	15	18	7
9. Teach children?	81.4	78	83	94	76	78	80	76	100	100
10. In school?	70.7	63	78	76	62	68	70	73	82	93
11. Were you?	90.3	88	93	94	86	90	92	88	91	100
12. Bible is . . .										
a. myths?	47.8	53	41	47	44	48	48	64	45	29
b. true?	36.3	38	34	12	25	34	45	39	45	93
c. too religious?	26.9	35	18	18	27	42	20	24	18	14
d. ancient history?	26.9	31	22	24	24	30	25	39	36	7
e. right & wrong?	46.9	46	47	35	39	52	38	52	64	79
f. comfort?	43.7	35	52	24	34	44	38	55	64	86
13. In church?										
a. last week	23.7	20	26	24	19	16	35	30	27	21
b. last month	13.1	9	17	24	13	18	13	6	9	14
c. last year	25.3	23	27	24	25	30	15	21	45	21
d. long ago	33.9	42	25	24	39	34	38	27	18	36
e. never	4.1	5	3	6	4	2	2	9	0	7
No. of respondents	244	124	121	17	79	50	40	33	11	14

f. *Comments on the Results of the Survey*

1. As for Bible knowledge, the best answered questions were:

Best known Bible facts	
the name of Jesus' mother	99%
where Adam and Eve lived	95% (1990), 90% (1992)
the 5000 were fed with bread and fish	93%
Noah was connected with the flood	90% (1990), 86% (1992)

The next range was:

Less well-known Bible facts	
The Good Samaritan was robbed	77%
Jesus was born about 2000 years ago	76%
Jerusalem was the city where Jesus died	67%
The talking ass belonged to Balaam	64%
There are four Gospels	64%

It would have been preferable to have chosen questions that produced a wider range of results.

2. These results suggest a basic knowledge of the Bible in more than half the interviewees. We should notice, however, that one person in four did not know Jesus was born around 1900 or 2000 years ago, and that one in three did not know that Jesus died in Jerusalem or that there are four Gospels.

3. As for the evaluation of the Bible, there was no very significant difference between the 1990 and the 1992 results—except that the 1992 sample were a little more negative toward the Bible:

Opinions about the Bible	1990	1992
The Bible is full of myths and legends	41.7	47.8
The Bible is true.	43.1	36 3
The Bible is too religious for me.	22.9	26.9
The Bible is really just ancient history.	27.1	26.9
The Bible is good for telling you what's right and wrong.		46.9
The Bible is a great comfort when you're in trouble.	42.4	43.7

What I find most significant is that about half the population thinks the Bible is full of myths and legends, and half thinks that it is good for telling you what is right and wrong. A third of the population would go so far as to say that the Bible is 'true', while a quarter would say the Bible is too religious for them. That is to say, at one end of the spectrum is the third who believe in the truth of the Bible, and at the other end the quarter who say the Bible is really just ancient history and too religious for their taste. In between is almost half the population (46.7%) who want neither to write the Bible off nor to assent to it. On the assumption that all of those who said the Bible was too religious for them also said it was full of myths and legends, there is still a quarter of the population (25.8%) who don't want to say the Bible is full of myths and legends but don't want to say it is true either. And while 36.3% wanted to say the Bible is true, significantly more wanted to say it's good for telling you what is right and wrong (46.9%), and even that it's a great comfort when you're in trouble (43.7%).

4. It will be interesting to correlate these opinions with our findings on church going.

| | *Churchgoing in 1990 and 1992* | | | |
	1990	*cumulative*	1992	*cumulative*
last week	27.6		23.7	
last month	15.9	43.5	13.1	36.8
last year	36.6	80.1	25.3	62.1
long ago	17.9	98.0	33.9	96.0
never	2.1	100.0	4.1	100.0

These figures are in themselves very interesting. They show that in 1992 only 62% of our sample had been to church in the last year, compared with 80% in 1990. They show a 14% drop in church attendance in the previous week (from 27.6% to 23.7% of the sample), and a 30% drop in attendance over the previous month (from 36.6% to 25.3% of the sample). The number who said they had attended church in the last year had dropped by 22%, while the number of those who said it was 'long ago' that they last went to church rose by 89%.

These figures no doubt need further glossing, and should not be taken at their face value. For example, the figure for attendance 'last week' of 23.7% or 27.6% is out of range of the national average of 11% or so that we know from other surveys (though we did not distinguish going to church as a worshipper, for example, from attending a funeral). But they must mean something, and the pattern is certainly consistent.

As for the correlation between opinions on the Bible and churchgoing, some general relationships stand out. The number of people wanting to say that the Bible is 'true' is the same as those who say they went to church in the last month—though I can't be sure that they are exactly the same people. At least as interesting is the fact that many who went to church in the last year did not want to say that the Bible is good for telling you what is right and wrong or that it is a great comfort when you are in trouble. Whether it is 80% of the population who have been to church in the last year, as we found in 1990, or 62% as it was in 1992, either figure is considerably greater than the 47% for the Bible as a source of moral guidance or 42-43% for the Bible as a source of comfort. These figures suggest strongly, but unsurprisingly, that the highest level of esteem for the Bible correlates broadly with at least monthly churchgoing, and that those who last went to church more than a month ago vary in their esteem for the Bible: about a third of them believe in the Bible as a source of moral guidance and comfort, but two-thirds do not.

5. Next we can consider the results for the question about Bible reading. As with all such questions about behaviour, interviews do not tell us the *facts* about Bible-reading, but people's perception of those facts, or rather, what they are prepared to say to the interviewer. But that is itself a fact, and it's the best we can hope to do in a postmodern world (it was the best we could ever do, but we used to pretend that we had access to objective reality).

Bible Reading, in 1990 and 1992				
	1990	cumulative	1992	cumulative
last week	18.6		22.6	
last month	8.3	26.9	9.7	32.3
last year	18.6	45.5	13.7	46.0
long ago	50.0	95.5	46.0	92.0
never	5.5	100.0	8.1	100.0

A broad interpretation of these figures is not difficult. We can say that a fifth of the population claim to read the Bible at least once a week, a third at least once a month and a half at least once a year. How we should describe this level of Bible-reading is not so easy to determine, however. I think I should call all these people 'Bible-readers', and those who read it at least once a month 'active Bible-readers'. But I should not say that anyone who has not

read the Bible in the last year is *not* a Bible-reader. I don't believe
I have read any Shakespeare myself in the last year, but I should
be offended if someone said I was therefore not a Shakespeare-
reader. Biblical scholars and religious professionals are perhaps
not the best people to judge in this matter, for many of them have
the idea that Bible-reading properly so-called is a daily activity—
but that is a standard we would not dream of applying to any
other literature. We would, of course, expect to find newspaper-
readers reading every day, or at least a few times a week. We
should perhaps need to consider whether the Bible is more like a
newspaper than like Shakespeare.

Another way of expressing the results of the survey is to say
that there are somewhat fewer active Bible-readers than active
churchgoers in the population, but that 11 out of 12 people have
read the Bible at some time (19 out of 20 if we use the 1990 figure).

6. All these results are worth putting alongside a survey of religious beliefs in Britain, Ireland and the USA recently reported on
in the press, and undertaken by Andrew Greeley, a sociologist
from the University of Chicago.[5]

Religious Beliefs and Observances				
% believing in	Britain	USA	Irish Republic	Northern Ireland
God	69	94	95	95
That God is concerned personally with people	37	77	77	80
Life after death	55	78	80	78
Heaven	54	86	87	90
Religious miracles	45	73	73	77
Hell	28	71	53	74
The devil	28	47	49	69
That the Bible is the 'actual' or inspired word of God	44	83	78	81
Affiliated with a denomination	64	93	98	92
Attend service 2/3 times monthly	16	43	78	58
Have had an intense religious experience	28	33	22	24

Here are some comments on these figures from the report in *The
Guardian*:

5.   'Who says the nation is on its knees?', *The Guardian*, November 18,
1992, p. 2/10.

The British are not on the whole devout; yet they are not irreli-
gious... Seven out of 10 of us say we believe in God, more than
half believe in life after death and in heaven, more than two in five
believe in religious miracles and some kind of biblical inspiration...
Britain is not a country where religion is especially vigorous—
perhaps it never was: recent research casts doubt on the assumptions of a past 'golden age'. But neither is it a country where religion is dying.

Even among those professing no religion, 35 per cent believe in
life after death, 18 per cent 'feel close to God', and 19 per cent say
they have had an intense religious experience.

Perhaps the most interesting figures in this survey relate to differences between Britain and the USA, which alert us once again
to how narrow a sample of 'the modern world' we have taken in
our Sheffield survey. It is a pity that England, Scotland and Wales
have been lumped together in this survey, for there are very
marked differences among them. I feel that at the two points at
which this survey connects with our own, the figures may perhaps be compatible if the national differences are taken into
account.

In Greeley's survey, 16% of the British population say they
attend a church service two or three times monthly. This com-
pares with our 1992 figure of 36.8% who say they have attended
once in the last month, but it is hard to reconcile with the 23.7%
of our respondents who say they attended church in the last
week. More directly relevant to our present concern is the number saying they believe the Bible is the 'actual' or inspired word
of God—44% in Greeley's survey, compared with the 36% in ours
who said the Bible was 'true' (43% in 1990). Speaking for myself,
I have to say that the figure amazes me, and gives me a new sense
of importance in my professional career! If a third of the population or more thinks that the Bible is 'true' or 'God's word', I certainly don't have to justify the presence of a Department of Biblical Studies over against a Department of Nuclear Physics (how
many people believe in neutrons, I wonder?)—and all the more
so when I find that 83% of the population of the USA agrees.

7. I do not intend to explore the results of our survey in depth.
But you will see that all the questions were also analysed by sex
and by age of the respondents, and I thought it would be interesting to draw attention to just a few highlights.

Men and women had, perhaps a little surprisingly, virtually the same level of Bible knowledge (men, average score 78, women, 80). But only 61% of men had a Bible of their own, contrasted with 81% of women. Women read the Bible more, 36% in the last month, compared with 28% of men. Rather more women than men think the Bible should be taught in school (78% as against 63%). Men and women agree on the Bible as a source of moral guidance (46% and 47%), but more women than men find it a source of comfort (52% against 35%), and more men than women count it too religious for them (35% against 18%). Strangely, though, more men than women want to say it is 'true' (38% against 34%)—or perhaps not so strangely, if it is predominantly men who desire hard facts and closures. Women are more frequent churchgoers (43% as against 29% in the last month).

As for the age bands, Bible knowledge was, surprisingly, much the same across the spectrum, with the under-20s and 20s not inferior to the 40s or 70s. But Bible ownership increased steadily with age, and weekly Bible reading was noticeably less favoured by the under-40s. The younger age groups had a distinctly less favourable attitude to the Bible; for example, only 12% of under-20s said the Bible was true, and 25% of 20s, compared with 93% of over-70s and an average of 36% across the whole population. Yet, surprisingly, only 18% of the under-20s said the Bible was too religious for them (contrast 42% of the 30s). The under-20s and the 40s had the 'best' churchgoing record.

2. *Survey of the Bible in the Press*

Another way of assessing how the Bible is perceived by the public is to see how it is used and referred to in the public media.[6] I would have liked to see how the Bible is being used in the popular press (and I happen to know of a doctoral thesis that is being done on the religious ideas of the *Sun* newspaper), but the survey I have made is restricted to *The Guardian*, for six months of 1992. There is one good reason for this choice. Several of the quality newspapers are now available on CD-ROM, enabling the reader

---

6.   I found no study of this theme, though there is an interesting volume of essays, *Religion and the Media: An Introductory Reader* (ed. Chris Arthur; Cardiff: University of Wales Press, 1993) .

to search the entire files electronically. Of *The Times*, *The Independent* and *The Guardian*, I chose *The Guardian* more or less at random.

I simply typed the word 'Bible' as my keyword, and immediately had 153 'hits' of places where the word Bible was used in the newspaper during the period April to September 1992, each with the date, the headline of the article, and a note on whether it was a news story, an editorial or a book review. By clicking on an entry I could see the entire article on screen, and with a single keystroke could print out those that took my fancy.

As you can see, the survey was not hugely extensive, and it cannot claim to be wholly representative of the British press. And in its turn, the British press cannot be said to be representative of the views of the public at large. But I reckoned that many articles that mentioned the Bible would not have been written by religious professionals, and that I would consequently be in touch with a more public use of the Bible than what I am generally used to. What is more, I thought that the way in which the Bible was referred to in such a context might be influencing to some degree the way the public at large thinks about the Bible, even if only subliminally, and that it could be useful to see what kinds of images of the Bible were being projected.

1. The 'Bible' is a term often used without reference to the Bible! As often happens with computer searches, I found quite a number of references I didn't want—or didn't think I wanted, at first. I was quite surprised at how many books that are not the Bible itself could be called a 'bible'. *Glass's Guide* is the retail car industry's bible, Daniel T. Jones's *The Machine that Changed the World* is the car industry's bible on lean production, Rayden is the legal bible, Butterworth publishes the tax bible, the *Financial Times* is the businessman's bible (and so also is the Italian magazine *Class*), *The Face* is the bible of youth style, Tina Brown's *Vanity Fair* a society bible, *Iron John* has been embraced by men as their bible (so it is said), *Pravda* is the Communist Party's bible (still?), *Monthly Film Bulletin* is the film buff's bible, Le Corbusier's *Vers un architecture* became the bible for the modern movement, *The Sporting Life* is the punter's bible, M.F.K. Fisher's *The Art of Eating* (1963) has become the food critics' bible, Camra's *Good Beer Guide* is the bible of a certain kind of pub-goer, Stephen Hawking's *A*

Brief History of Time has become a secular bible in many homes, and *Grouse in Space and Time* will, we are assured, 'become a bible for future upland conservation'.

Now *The Guardian's* copy-editing style insists on a small 'b' for 'bible' in such usages, and generally manages to achieve its ideal. But what does this use of 'bible' with a small 'b' tell us about the Bible with a capital 'B'? I think the key element is the idea of authority. *Glass's Guide* tells second-hand car salespersons what the current market value of every model is; it sets the norms (even though, of course, it derives its own norms from outside itself, from the market prices). A tax bible tells you authoritatively what the law is, *The Sporting Life* reports authoritatively on the results of recent races and the form of the horses. There is also an air of exhaustiveness and completeness about a 'bible' (as with *Glass's Guide*, the *Financial Times* and *Monthly Film Bulletin*), perhaps also of inspiration, as with *The Face* and *Vanity Fair* and Le Corbusier. And there is undoubtedly also the idea of specialism: each trade or hobby or party has its lore as well as its law, and its bible is an enshrining of its peculiarities as well as a resource for trainee members. So a bible is educational, and a member of the guild has to become well versed in it. Finally, there is usually only one bible per subject area; a bible has pole position—and monopoly position. At first sight that might not seem true about the *Financial Times* and *Class*, which are both said to be the bible of the 'businessman'. But they surely do not compete for the allegiance of the 'businessman' in the same field, not unless the *FT* has taken to producing fashion supplements and *Class* prints the latest commodities prices.

This may all seem beside the point for the Bible (with a capital 'B') in the modern world. But what if we allowed that every time a *Guardian* reader encounters 'bible' in this sense, he or she is being given an implicit model for how to regard the Bible itself—a model that may be all the more persuasive precisely because it is implicit? I think that is certainly what happens.

2. I will pass over quickly the more purely factual references in the newspaper to the Bible, as to the Vinegar Bible in the church of Cartmel in Cumbria, which has 'vinegar' instead of 'vineyard' —the fault of 'some poor monk, probably wrecked on real mead'. This fact is, as the journalist says, reviewing a guide to real ale

pubs, a 'piece of premium-strength trivia'.[7] In the Food and Drink pages for April 18, 'Pass over the Matzos' explains the origin of the Passover food customs by reference to 'an order in the Bible'.[8] In these months too, the world's oldest bound book was put on display in Cairo, a fourth-century copy of the Book of Psalms in Coptic.[9] Gabriel Josipovici, professor of English at Sussex and 'student of the Bible' has published a collection of essays that are distinctly not postmodernist.[10] Reviewing an oratorio by the seventeenth-century Italian composer Stradella about Salome, the music critic Edward Greenfield writes that 'the main purpose of these church entertainments was to heighten the impact of Bible stories'.[11]

3. And I will pass over the mere quotations from the Bible, for example, 'It takes a lot of courage in Germany to kick against the pricks, as they say in the Bible'.[12] (I hadn't thought Paul was being commended for his courage in kicking against the pricks [Acts 26.14], but that is another matter!)

4. I come now to some citations that suggest how the Bible is being regarded in the popular culture. The first I will mention is that the Bible is a benchmark of size. It is a long book, but it is one book. To shut him up, Evelyn Waugh bet Randolph Churchill £10 that he couldn't read the Bible in a fortnight. To actually write the Bible would be a gargantuan, ridiculously enormous or impossible task. The editor of the *Oxford Companion to the English Language*, Tom McArthur, describes being invited to produce the volume. 'It was mission impossible, a monstrous project, appalling and appealing, like crossing a trackless waste, being asked

7. David Newnham, 'Paperback digest', *The Guardian*, August 22, 1992, p. 25.

8. Helen Franks, 'Pass over the Matzos', *The Guardian*, April 18, 1992, p. 17.

9. Deborah Pugh, 'World's oldest book is unveiled', *The Guardian*, September 14, 1992, p. 8.

10. John Lanchester, 'The persuasive purist', *The Guardian*, July 2, 1992, p. 26.

11. Edward Greenfield, 'Sacred origins of a sensual Salome', *The Guardian*, June 4, 1992, p. 31.

12. Robert McCrum, 'Comrades in exile. Four emigrants to the GDR watch German capitalism dismantle all they have worked for and believed in', *The Guardian*, June 27, 1992, p. 19.

to write the Bible, putting one's head into a lion's mouth or...
going to sea in a sieve.'[13]

5. The Bible is a popular book, a best-seller. Its sales are a
benchmark for sales figures for other titles. 'Benjamin Spock will
be 89 tomorrow, the grandfather of 30 million baby bibles, whose
sales are bettered only by the Bible itself (a book notoriously
ambivalent about mothers and children, whatever the Pope may
say).'[14]

6. The Bible is an arbiter of style. Toni Morrison, the black
American writer who has been called by the New York Times
'the nearest thing America has to a national novelist', is noted for
the mixture of the lyrical and the simple in her writing. Her first
novel, *The Bluest Eye* (1970), opens with the sentence, 'Nuns go
by as quiet as lust, and drunken men with sober eyes sing in the
lobby of the Greek hotel'—a sentence that, as the reviewer says,
'bursts with lovely imminence'. Speaking of her writing, Morrison
says, 'I love speech, and I've always thought the sources of it
were familial—listening to the way my parents spoke to each
other, when they felt it necessary to be Biblical or simple, how
they adjusted language'.[15]

7. The Bible is a benchmark for moral values. John Patten, the
then education minister, thought the churches should have more
to say about damnation for those in our society who choose
wrong rather than right. But a correspondent writes that 'If Mr
Patten really wants the church to preach damnation more effec-
tively he had better study his Bible. Those who[m] Jesus and the
prophets condemned were the wealthy, the powerful and the
hypocrites. The poor, the thieves and the prostitutes—more likely
to repent—were to be first into paradise.'[16] Indeed, says Steve
Parish, Vicar of St Ann's, Warrington, John Patten's conser-
vatism is founded on the concept of self-reliance, 'a concept that
flies against the two great Bible themes of trusting of God and

13. John Ezard, 'A reluctant Pope for correct English', *The Guardian*,
September 12, 1992, p. 27.

14. C.P.D., 'Weekend Birthdays', *The Guardian*, May 2, 1992, p. 28.

15. 'A Terrible Privacy', *The Guardian*, April 18, 1992, p. 4.

16. David Haslam, 'Eye of a needle', *The Guardian*, April 21, 1992, p. 20.

looking to the interests of others'. Self-reliance may be the broad way to hell, rather than a political and personal virtue.[17]

8. Reading the Bible is a sign of normality and social conformity. In Liberia, following the civil war in which children were recruited into the National Patriotic Front,

> teenage killers, some of whom admit to having butchered up to 50 people, read the Bible and are encouraged to pray every day as part of a rehabilitation programme. When they leave, they will be given a certificate which recognises that they are 'ready to rejoin civilised society'.[18]

Or take the case of Marion Berry, the flamboyant black mayor of Washington who was caught snorting cocaine in a sting by the FBI and gaoled. Now he is making a political comeback, 'portraying himself as a reformed, God-fearing character who ha[s] paid his debt to society':

> Through an assiduous campaign running over several months— in which he has attended numerous church services, frequently quoted from the Bible, dressed modestly, and led a voter registration drive—Mr Barry has attempted to persuade voters that he is a changed man.[19]

It is fascinating to see what you need to do to be taken as a sober citizen.

9. The Bible encapsulates a moral principle that is yet again proved to be valid. In a BBC documentary film, a German woman discovers she is the child of a SS general, exterminator of the 45,000 Jews of Riga, known as the Butcher of Riga. She travels to Latvia and speaks to one of the few survivors. Isaac Kleiman tries to comfort her: 'It says in the Bible, "No son is responsible for his father's actions"'.[20] And the reviewer comments, 'He's changed

17. Steve Parish, 'Face to Faith: A sermon on hell for John Patten', *The Guardian*, May 16, 1992, p. 26.

18. Mark Husband, 'Ghosts of civil war haunt Liberia's child soldiers. Former fighters are trying to exorcise the killing fields', *The Guardian*, April 13, 1992, p. 10.

19. Simon Tisdall, 'Disgraced mayor makes comeback', *The Guardian*, September 16, 1992, p. 8.

20. I suppose that the reference is to Jer. 31.29, 'In those days people will no longer say, "The fathers have eaten sour grapes, and the children's teeth

His tune since then. I understood that He visited the sins of the fathers upon the children under the third and fourth generation and so, I suspect, did Renate. She is 50. She is not married. She has no children.' You need to be something of a biblical critic yourself to recognize the interesting move that is being made here: the negation of the biblical text is actually done from within the Bible itself.

10. The Bible contains moral principles that are no longer valid. In a very powerful extract from his book, *An Evil Cradling* (1992), Brian Keenan, the Irishman taken prisoner in Beirut, tells of terrible beatings he endured from one of his guards:

> I wondered how many more times before I could contain myself no longer and try to wreak havoc on him. I remembered as I lay there how he had often quoted a phrase from the Koran, one that is copied from the Christian Bible, 'An eye for an eye and a tooth for a tooth'.

But this immediate desire for revenge was supplanted by a new feeling:

> I felt a new and tremendous kind of strength flooding me. The more I was beaten the stronger I seemed to become. It was not strength of arm, nor of body, but a huge determination never to give in to these men, never to show fear, never to cower in front of them. To take what violence they meted out to me and stand and resist and not allow myself to be humiliated.[21]

The Bible is represented here by one text that is taken as being typical of the whole, and its incitement to revenge is rejected in favour of a different principle, of non-retaliation, not on pacifist or what you could call Christian grounds, but as a stronger and more effective weapon against hatred.

11. The Bible is an antique text, and not surprisingly mistaken at times. Take the case of the value of pi. 'The Bible (1 Kings 7:23) got it rather wrong, and called it 3', when it gave the dimensions of the molten sea in the temple as 10 cubits in diameter and 30 in

---

are set on edge"' (NIV). This modern-world use of the text is an interesting example of what is called in the trade 'over-realized eschatology'.

21. Brian Keenan, 'Rape', *The Guardian*, September 12, 1992, p. 9.

circumference.[22] It is actually 3.121592 and so on, though in schools we usually make do with 22 over 7. It is interesting that the 1 Kings figures are called 'getting it rather wrong' and that this 'error' is ascribed to the 'Bible'—as though the Bible itself has a responsibility for all its contents, as though somehow it is expected that the Bible ought to be 'right' over such matters (as if it made that claim), and as if, in any case, no compromises could be made over the question of what 'right' is when it comes to the value of pi. After all, it was only in 1991 that the Chudnovsky brothers calculated pi to 2.16 billion decimal places, so was everyone 'wrong' before that? And why stop at 2.16 billion? Aren't you just exposing yourself to a charge of 'error' from the next number-cruncher that comes along?

12. The Bible and Bible-reading are part of life's rich tapestry, often in exotic locations, like the description of the queue of people waiting to see Ghana's political leader Jerry Rawlings:

> Chiefs in flowing robes, sandals and elaborate gold rings, powerful queen mothers, elderly men in pinstripe suits, and an eager evangelist using the time to exhort people to read the Bible, wait patiently.[23]

There was an evocative account too of a blind Egyptian preacher, with his battered Braille Bible. And one read that the ritual of exorcism, introduced into the Catholic church in the sixteenth century, is accompanied by readings from the Bible.

13. The Bible and Bible-reading is a sign of culture, and token of a vanishing culture. Said the historian G.M. Trevelyan, 'In the seventeenth century, Members of Parliament quoted from the Bible; in the eighteenth and nineteenth centuries from the classics; in the twentieth century from nothing at all'.[24] The two books that all Australians should read are the Bible and the thoughts of Chairman Mao, according to the maverick editor Francis James.

22. Tim Radford, 'Babylon belittled by brothers' pi in the sky', *The Guardian*, August 29, 1992, p. 6.

23. Victoria Brittain, 'Ghana's leader tries to buck Africa's election trend', *The Guardian*, July 4, 1992, p. 10.

24. Keith Thomas, 'Great patriot who sat dazed in the ruins of the world' (review of a biography by David Cannadine), *The Guardian*, September 24, 1992, p. 24.

The Bible is one of Fidel Castro's classics. Obituaries not infre-
quently remark on their subjects' familiarity with the Bible:
Flintoff, for example, read the Bible and the Koran; Xenakis cited
the Bible; Franz Weber-Most took the teachings of the Bible and
the Buddha as his guides. The disappearance of Bible-reading
('the Bible is largely unread') is a sign of the de-Christianizing of
the nation and an argument for the dis-establishment of the
Church of England, says an Anglican bishop.[25] If you are deplor-
ing the disappearance of culture in our times, you are likely to
remark that the television game show is the late twentieth century's 'answer to Elizabethan theatre and the Guttenburg [*sic*]
Bible'—twin symbols of culture, it appears.[26] And we can be sure
the Bible has earned its cultural laurels when we discover it is one
of the recommended books for teaching and testing in schools
under the (though Shakespeare, interestingly enough, is the only
author whose presence in the classroom is compulsory).[27]

14. The Bible is an earthy book. Convent girls 'know where all
the rude bits in the Bible are'.[28] The rest of us just know there *are*
rude bits.

15. And here, finally, is a reference to the Bible I could ex-
pound on for ages. On the gardening page, a reader writes:

> I have a tiny pool in a walled garden. The pool teems with frog
> and toad tadpoles and this summer the garden is alive with the
> result. Remembering the plague of frogs in the Bible, I'm won-
> dering whether I should discourage them, or whether they will
> eventually cull themselves.[29]

How close to this gardener's consciousness is the biblical text?, I
ask myself. What primal anxiety does the recollection of the biblical plague conjure up? Does the Bible capture in words humanity's death wish and cosmic anxiety, with tales of a universal

25. Colin Buchanan, 'Not a fit state to be in', *The Guardian*, September 11,
1992, p. 19.

26. Robert Pryce, 'Soccer Diary', *The Guardian*, April 25, 1992, p. 16.

27. James Meikle, 'Shakespeare and Spike Milligan on original list of
approved authors', *The Guardian*, September 10, 1992, p. 3.

28. Carmel Fitzsimons, 'Sex, salvation and a hellfire editor' (Cristina
Odone, the editor of the *Catholic Herald*), *The Guardian*, September 21, 1992,
p. 25.

29. Hilary Applegate, 'Growbag', *The Guardian*, September 19, 1992, p. 35.

flood, a last day, a pit of fire, a shaking of the foundations—and a plague of frogs? The Bible is certainly in the modern world if you can't escape it even in a tiny pool of tadpoles in a walled garden. Hang on a minute, what was that about a walled garden? I'm getting mixed messages here (cf. Song 4.12!).

How can this cornucopia of biblical reference in the pages of *The Guardian* be summarized, and what does this collection of data *mean*?

1. I have the image of an authority that is no longer perceived as authoritative but that is quite esteemed still, like Mrs Beeton's *The Book of Household Management* or Aristotle *On the Art of Poetry* or Johnson's *Dictionary* or the ninth edition of the *Encyclopaedia Britannica*—like a classic, in fact.

2. It is a common possession of the culture: everyone can be relied on to know what the Bible is and roughly how long it is, to know that it is the best-selling book.

3. It is recognized as a sign of civilization. It is for this reason that, on *Desert Island Discs*,[30] you get the Bible and Shakespeare on your desert island, whether or not you like it, because you are expected to want to retain some trappings of civilization, even if you do not dress for dinner.

4. Because it is so venerable, a little fun at its expense is not thought out of order. *Guardian* readers are not going to give up reading the Bible because it got the value of pi 'wrong'.

5. The Bible is still perceived as a foundation of moral values, or at least as enshrining in memorable forms universal values. This is only the case, it must be noted, when the Bible coincides with contemporary values. No one says, Ethnic cleansing is of course a biblical idea; nor do you see references to Deuteronomy 22.5 in advertisements for women's clothing ('A woman shall not wear anything that pertains to a man, nor shall a man put on a woman's garment; for whoever does these things is an abomination to

30. A long-running BBC radio programme in which each week a celebrity is invited to choose eight music records he or she would choose to take to a desert island; parts of the records are played and the interviewee reminisces. The interviewee is allowed to choose one luxury, but does not have to consider whether to take the Bible and Shakespeare; they are automatically provided.

the LORD your God'). If you do not agree with something the Bible says, you probably will simply not refer to it. Just occasionally you enter into dispute with a famous biblical text that continues to have influence on you and that you need to exorcise (so with Brian Keenan).

6. The Bible is the property of the culture generally; it is not accessed through the church—or the academy, for that matter.[31] No one in citing it says, Of course, I may be wrong in my interpretation, or, Perhaps this goes against the correct interpretation, and I should check it out with my vicar or ring up the Department of Biblical Studies in Sheffield for an authoritative view. Everyone thinks they have the right to read and understand the Bible for themselves. And for myself—I am determined to butt into the conversation at this point—I should rather they do that, getting it wildly wrong if needs be, rather than have an authorized interpretation presided over by popes or vicars or professors.[32] If faith cometh by hearing and hearing by the word of God and if the Bible has anything to do with the word of God, then the culture has got it right and the church has got it wrong: the plain Scripture, without ecclesiastical gloss or control, must be in the hands of the common reader. I take my stand with Tyndale (though not with his anti-Jewish sentiments) when he wrote:

31. When my class on the Bible in the Modern World assembles again, I shall turn them loose on a cutting from the *Independent on Sunday*, 25 September, 1994, p. 8, Peter Wilby's article, 'Jesus beats Marx for Labour politicians'. He gives the result of a survey showing that in a poll of 100 Labour MPs the Bible was mentioned as an important literary influence even above Karl Marx. In 1994 top of the poll was Robert Tressell (author of *The Ragged Trousered Philanthropists* [London: Lawrence & Wishart, 1955]) and R.H. Tawney (author of, most famously, *Religion and the Rise of Capitalism: An Historical Study* [Holland Memorial Lectures, 1922; London: J. Murray, 1926]), with the Bible and Marx in third and fourth places. In a similar poll in 1975 the Bible was not mentioned in the top ten places, though it was fifth in a poll in 1962 and second (after John Ruskin) in a poll in 1906. I am grateful to John Lyons, a graduate student in the Department, for bringing me the cutting. A fuller account of the survey was published by Steve Platt and Julia Gallagher, under the title 'From Bevan to the Bible', *New Statesman and Society*, September 30, 1994, pp. 22-24.

32. No disrespect to any of these groups intended, of course; that's why I put 'professors' in there as well!

Moreover, because the kyngedome of heaven, which is the scripture and worde of God, maye be so locke vp, that he which readeth
or heareth it, cannot vnderstonde it: as Christ testifieth how that
the Scribes and Pharisees had so shut it vp…that their Iewes
which thought them selves within, were yet so locked out, and
are to this daye that they can vnderstonde no sentence of the
scripture vnto their salvacion, though they can reherse the textes
every where and dispute therof as sottelye as the popysche doc-
toures of dunces darcke learninge, wihich with their sophistrye,
sarved vs, as the Pharises dyd the Iewes.[33]

None of what we have been hearing tonight from the Bible in
the press is the Bible as it is known by the devoted Bible-reader
or the biblical scholar. Believers in the divine inspiration of the
Bible are aghast or at least disappointed that the Bible is not
more revered than it is. But they would be wrong, I think, to fear
that the Bible is treated in popular culture as simply a book
among other books. Of course it *is* a book, and you can read it
and understand it (or fail to understand it) like any other book.
But the Bible has a unique status in our popular culture. So too
has Shakespeare, of course, but its special status is different from
that of the Bible—in ways that would be worth exploring further. What interests me is that the issue of truth is not up front
with Shakespeare; that is surprising, in a way, since the 'truth' or
'insight' of the Shakespeare corpus might well be esteemed even
above its dramatic or verbal qualities. With the Bible, 'truth' is
not the only item on the agenda, but it is certainly a fundamental
question, and the popular culture has not got that wrong.

33. 'W.T. vnto the Reader', in *The New Testament Translated by William Tyndale, 1534* (a reprint of the 1534 edition) (ed. N. Hardy Wallis; Cambridge: Cambridge University Press, 1938), p. 3.

Chapter 4

THE BIBLE AND THE CHURCH

Looking about the modern world for signs of the Bible's presence, we inevitably come to the church as an area where we can encounter the Bible and its use. Many people both inside and outside the church would think of this first as the natural locus of the Bible in the modern world, and some indeed would think of it first and last. That is why I deferred this topic to the end, because I wanted in this course of lectures to emphasize that the church has no exclusive rights to the Bible, and that the Bible belongs to the society as a whole, not just, perhaps even not primarily, to the church.

But now that we come to the topic, where shall we start? As with the other lectures, I felt that we should have some data in our hands before we started to generalize. None of the books I knew on the subject, from James Smart's *The Strange Silence of the Bible in the Church*[1] to James Barr's *The Bible in the Modern World*[2] (no relation to the present lectures) and Robert Carroll's *Wolf in the Sheepfold*[3] had done any research on the facts, the actual state of affairs. They relied on anecdotal evidence that supported their views, striking individual pieces of knowledge that they wove into a pattern. I haven't done much better, but at least I had what is called in the trade a research methodology.

1. James D. Smart, *The Strange Silence of the Bible in the Church: A Study in Hermeneutics* (London: SCM Press, 1970).

2. James Barr, *The Bible in the Modern World* (London: SCM Press, 1973). I have made my title *The Bible and the Modern World* so as not to steal Barr's, but it means exactly the same thing.

3. Robert P. Carroll, *Wolf in the Sheepfold: The Bible as a Problem for Christianity* (London: SPCK, 1991).

1. *A Survey of the Use of the Bible in Churches*

I decided that we needed to have some information about how the Bible is actually used in churches, some information gleaned by observers and not too reliant on the testimony of the church people and leaders themselves. I knew already that churches have views about the Bible and what they should be doing with the Bible, and I suspected that their ideals might skew the way they evaluated what was actually going on. So I sent my trusty BMW class out, three by three, into the highways and byways of Sheffield, with never a purse or scrip among them, to be my eyes and ears in the churches. To tell the truth, *they* decided, for this segment of their course on the Bible in the Modern World, which churches in Sheffield they wanted to visit, what they would look for when they were there, who they would talk to, and what they would be aiming to find out. I laid upon them no greater burden (I'm sorry about all the biblical language, but it gets to you in the end, doesn't it?) than that no one should visit a church of their own tradition, and that the class as a whole should try to cover a wide but balanced range of churches. It was impossible, with only 14 groups of surveyors, to weight the survey fairly, so that, for example, the larger denominations would be visited by more groups; we knew in advance that this would not be a survey as quantifiable as the street survey, and that it would be quite impressionistic. But we felt we had to start somewhere, and it was very exciting having the feeling that we were *starting* something that as far as we knew hadn't been done before.

These were the congregations we visited: a Roman Catholic parish church, the Anglican cathedral, the Salvation Army, a United Reformed church, a Methodist church, a Christadelphian ecclesia, a house church, an Apostolic Pentecostal church, a congregation of Jehovah's Witnesses, a Christian Science church, a Christian Brethren assembly, a Unitarian church, an orthodox synagogue and a reform synagogue. We were there, with the prior permission of the leaders of the congregations in every case, as non-partisan observers, not as critics or judges. Every student, churchgoer or not, was to some extent in alien territory, and it took some personal courage in some cases to get through the front door. But this sense of distance from what was being observed was of course essential for the exercise. It proved impossible, not surprisingly, for students to maintain their observer status once they had finished their visits, and to refrain from judging and criticizing what they saw. But that was not a fault; rather, it was their ethical response to their experience. We expect reporters in Bosnia to give us the facts (as they see them, naturally) and to maintain an air of neutrality in their broadcast; but we would think the worse of them as human beings if we had reason to believe that they were personally unaffected by the human misery they were seeing every day at first hand.

The class began its work by preparing a set of notes for all the groups, to enable them to report systematically on the Bible in the church. They suggested what the groups should look for in the church building and in the service, and what questions they should ask of the church leader with whom they had arranged a meeting separate from the service. Here are the guidelines they prepared:

THE BIBLE IN THE MODERN WORLD

Church Visits, November 1 and 8, 1992

1. *Checklist for Observation and Assessment*

General

1. How will we record the service? Tape-record? (? permission). Photocopy hymns, liturgical texts? Write down free prayers, sermon?
2. How will the recording be shared among our group?

Bible

1. Is the Bible openly visible when entering the church? Where?
2. Are there Bibles in the pews?
3. Are there any other visible biblical words or images (e.g. stained glass, posters, banners)?
4. Do the congregation bring their own Bibles?

Readings

1. Which version of the Bible is used in the service?
2. Is the Bible quoted explicitly? Is it read? Are readings from OT or NT or both?
3. Is there any kind of ritual involved in the use of the Bible?

---

4.   Do people stand or sit for the readings?
5.   Are any texts besides the Bible read?
6.   Do the readings use inclusive language?
7.   Who reads?

Songs and Hymns
1.   What songs or hymns are sung?
2.   Do the songs and hymns contain biblical references?

Prayers
1.   Is the Lord's Prayer used? the grace? other portions of the Bible?
2.   Is the Bible used explicitly in spontaneous prayer?
3.   Are there set prayers? Do they use biblical language or references?

Sermon
1.   How often is the Bible directly referred to in the sermon?
2.   Does the sermon start with a text?
3.   Does the sermon use a text as a base, an anchor to which it constantly returns, or is a text used as a jumping off point for the beginning of the sermon?
4.   Is the text interpreted as relevant to today? Is it related to current issues?

Communion
1.   Is the Bible quoted in the communion service?

2. *Interview Questions for the Minister or Leader*

1.   In this church, how typical is what we have seen and heard?
2.   Do Bible readings in services follow any kind of lectionary or are they chosen to support the message given in the sermon? Do the readings determine the message or the message the reading?
3.   Do you have group Bible study in the church?
4.   Why does your church use the version of the Bible it does?
5.   Is the Apocrypha used in church services?
6.   What is your view / your church's view of or attitude towards the Bible?
       Is it essentially divinely inspired or a human document?
       Is it a history book or 'living word'?
       Is it out of date or applicable to today's world?
       Is the Bible used as a source of moral guidance?

Does it hold an answer for every situation arising in today's world?

7.   What sort of issues/questions do you feel the Bible addresses today (e.g. divorce)? Are there moral/political/social questions which the Bible does not address some how? Is the Bible your primary resource for dealing with moral issues? Is it appropriate to use the Bible in this sort of context? If so, how?

8.   Do members of the congregation read the Bible privately?

9.   What kind of biblical knowledge do you expect in the people you preach to?

10.   Do you view academic study of the Bible (including the biblical languages) as either useful or relevant? Can you see any way academic study such as is done in our depart ment could contribute to the life of your church?

11.   Do the children receive Bible teaching? In what form?

12.   Is the Bible used as a tool for prayer? How? Is it quoted in prayer?

13.   How does your church deal with relationships between scientific discoveries and biblical accounts (e.g. creation, evolution)?

14.   Does the church have a 'constitution'? Is there a biblical basis for this?

15.   Does the Bible play any part in the decision-making processes of the church? How?

16.   Does the congregation converse with you on biblical matters raised in the sermon? Do they always agree with your interpretation? Are your interpretations seen as author itative?

17.   Do you find certain passages in the Bible problematic? If so, how do you deal with them?

18.   Have there been any changes in the use of the Bible in your church?
       Would you want to make any?

19.   Do you give different parts of the Bible more importance than others? If so, why?

Each of the student groups prepared a written report of their church visit, and presented a short summary of it to the class as a whole. Each group then had to append to their report a one-page appraisal of the findings of the whole set of groups. In the final exam, for which the questions were designed and set in co-operation with the class, students had an opportunity to return to the topic and offer their more mature reflections on the whole exercise.

What follows is the essay I would have written if I had been sitting that exam.

1. The most striking thing for me was that, on the whole, it was the non-mainstream churches that gave the greatest weight to the Bible. In the Christian Science church, for example, there was nothing except readings from the Bible and from Mary Baker Eddy's *Science and Health*. There was no interpretation, no exposition, no application—of either text. It was textuality in its purest form. At the Kingdom Hall of Jehovah's Witnesses, there was indeed exposition of the biblical passages, affirmation that biblical prophecies are being fulfilled today and that the Bible covers every circumstance in life. But the dominant impression was of the supremacy of the Bible: the homily was a tissue of biblical quotations, and there was a study sheet on the theme for the day, containing 64 biblical references to the topic 'Jehovah's use of foolishness'. The Christadelphian ecclesia, very strait-laced and biblically based (one student confessed ruefully she hadn't realized that this would be a 'skirt and hat job'), had a 40-minute sermon with continuous reference to the Bible, a weekly Bible study, and the assurance that the Bible was applicable to 90% of today's issues. I have to admit one exception to my generalization, though. The Unitarian church is not, I suppose, what you would call mainstream Christianity, and yet it gave the least place to the Bible of all the churches visited: there the Bible was referred to only once in the sermon, by way of being blamed for the Reformation and the Protestant work ethic that have led to the cult of 'success' and the feeling of inadequacy that threatens too many people.

On the other hand, the strongest impression I gained of the use of the Bible from the report of the visit to the Anglican cathedral was of the notice our intrepid reporters observed: 'Warning: All items in this cathedral are electronically security-coded. Philippians 4:19 And my God will meet all your needs.' There were no Bibles in the pews, nor on the lectern. The reason given was that they didn't want them stolen—which rang a little hollow to our group when they observed that there were plenty of prayer-books in the pews. In the Catholic church, while there were readings from the Bible in the service, our group carried away a strong impression that the Bible is regarded as incomplete and as standing in need of interpretation by the church. The community shaped the Bible, and therefore the community must interpret it. Though the church had a prayer group that based its prayer on the Bible, our students were told that reading the Bible for personal devotion was not a very Catholic thing to do. The Methodist church had readings from Old and New Testament, and a sermon with many biblical references that were related to helping individual hearers live as Christians. But when asked whether the Bible was a divinely inspired or a human book, the church leader said, Both—and gave the same answer to the question, Is it a historical book or a living book? and Is it out of date or applicable? At the Brethren assembly, though there was much biblical allusion, the hymns seemed to be at least as important as the Bible. While it was said that the Bible was divinely inspired, it was also said to give only general guidance to Christians today, not necessarily specific direction, and the church leaders said they expected little by way of Bible knowledge from the congregation.

I need to interject that none of these observations is my own. I am reporting on what my students said. Perhaps they got it wrong. Perhaps also the church leaders got it wrong. Perhaps none of the services was typical of that church. Perhaps, perhaps. But facts are not 'realities out there'. They are only agreed perceptions. What is important here is that if a group of three intelligent students got such and such an impression when they had been carefully trained to observe these churches, and when they were doing their best to be non-partisan—what does intention or 'actuality' matter? This is what they brought away with them, and it has its own actuality.

2. My second observation was that biblical scholarship and biblical criticism seemed to have had no significant effect on the reading and interpretation of the Bible in the churches. To be sure, one of the sermons referred to the fact that the Epistle to the Hebrews was not by Paul, and another said something about science and the Bible. Again, there may well be other places, other churches, where things are different, and I'm not claiming universal validity for our survey. But you would have thought, wouldn't you, that scholarly views about the Bible might have

come to the surface somewhere in Sheffield one Sunday morning in February.

I can only conclude that biblical criticism is perceived as irrelevant to the church. This may well not be the fault of the church, or the fault of the scholars. There may well be no fault around at all. It may be, at the end of the day, that biblical criticism is indeed irrelevant to the church—and rightly so. But, as things stand, both the church and the Academy are complicit in an agreement that biblical criticism *is* what the church needs, and its ministers are trained in it at vast expense—though to little purpose, as it seems.

3. The Bible is a Christian book and it supports Christian theology. Any evidence that is to the contrary, or that seems to be the contrary, is ignored.

3. *Thoughts on the Use of the Bible in the Church*

I need to make my own position clear here. Hitherto in these lectures I have been speaking as a professor of biblical studies, a hireling of the state who is submissive to the academic ideals of fairmindedness, critical distance and rigorous following of the evidence no matter where it may lead. I am not a servant of the church, and I am not its spokesman. I can say nothing that binds anyone's conscience (thankfully). And I am not changing my tune now. I am not a lover of the church, having always found that article of the (falsely so-called) the most difficult to swallow. But I am a well-wisher, and am happy to offer my freelance consultative advice to the church. I will not say, For what it is worth, for I never found the church that paid me what I think I am worth on the open market; let's just say, On a goodwill basis. I just need to make clear that I am not being paid to serve the special interests of the church or of the Christian religion, and that I undertake tasks like advising the church about its use of the Bible purely in my spare time and as a hobby.

1. I begin on a somewhat negative note. It is that if the church insists on control of the interpretation of the Bible, it will find itself on the losing side. For the tendency of things, on the interpretative front, as I outlined in the first lecture, is to move away from the concept of determinate meanings, and to locate meaning

not forceful assertion,
but a hopeful assertion

in the activity of the reader. No church, no institution, can control all the possible meanings that readers come up with; it can only hope to assert that such and such is the meaning that you must all adopt. But when its members get to realize that texts are not like that, texts in general I mean, the church that insists on controlling interpretation is going to be badly wrongfooted.

2. But there is a more positive way of making this point. If the church can accept the idea of a plurality of interpretations, it will unleash the creative potentiality of its members. My opinion is that hierarchical and authoritarian churches, those where there is a strong central government or where the life of the individual congregation revolves about the minister or pastor, are almost certainly wasting their most valuable resource, the talents of the congregation as a whole. 'Letting a hundred flowers blossom and a hundred schools of thought contend is the policy for promoting the progress of the arts and the sciences'—so Mao Zedong;[4] but also, will you not agree, the progress of theology and the church.

3. There is the matter of critical distance from the text. As we saw in the survey of the churches, the development of biblical criticism has left the church almost entirely untouched. Maybe it doesn't matter so much that the church is unaware that the Pastoral Epistles were probably not written by Paul or that the Pentateuch was not written by Moses. What does matter is that the church and its people are in possession of an entirely false picture of the connection of the Bible with historical actuality. They do not know, for example, that biblical critics agree that it is hard to be sure that any saying ascribed to Jesus was acutally spoken by him, that we have no certain access to the historical Jesus, and that the Jesus of the Gospels is a character in a book, not a real person. I would like to leave it an open question how crucial such knowledge is for the life of the church. But it *is* knowledge—or, more often, the Socratean knowing that we do not know—and one thing is certain: people put a lot of store by knowledge, even bad and defective knowledge. The question is: Why is the church being kept in ignorance of what is known in the Academy about the Bible? How can church leaders possibly think it profits the

4. Mao Zedong, *Quotations from Chairman Mao Tse-Tung* (Peking: Foreign Languages Press, 2nd edn, 1967), §32.

Christian community to be kept out of the picture, even about elementary facts about the Bible?

4. The church, in my opinion, should reconsider its traditional language about the Bible—which isn't just language, but the expression of attitudes that shape, to some extent, its behaviour and decisions. I take the case of the concept of the Bible as the word of God. Not many people know that this is not itself a biblical idea. Neither Genesis nor the Psalms, for example, and not even the Gospels, say this about themselves, nor do other parts of the Bible say it about them. It is the prophets, and the prophets almost exclusively, who claim to be speaking the word of God, and it is in the prophetic books that the concept is at home. When the phrase occurs in the New Testament, it is never in reference to a writing, but typically to preaching. The 'word of God' is something that is 'spoken' or 'proclaimed', never 'written'. The idea that the Bible, a written text, should be called 'the word of God' is the invention of fallible human men. (I use the term 'men' deliberately; it blows the mind to think what Christian doctrine would look like if Nicaea and Chalcedon had been the decisions of women. But it would still be fallible.)

Just because the idea of the Bible as the 'word of God' is the invention of fallible humans does not mean it is wrong, of course; but it does mean that it is not beyond criticism. And a set of key questions the church should have on its agenda at the present moment are, Do we want this language any more? What unwanted freight does it carry along with it?, and Could it be that one of the reasons the church has perpetuated this phrase is because it serves the church's craving for power to have charge of this 'word of God'? It was interesting that 44% of the British public and 83% of Americans in the questionnaire I cited yesterday said they believed that the Bible is the 'actual' or inspired word of God; that can only be evidence that there has been a huge selling campaign over the decades for this particular description of the Bible that comes, let me say it again, from somewhere other than the Bible.

The difficulties with the term are two: (1) It screens out the human authorship of the Bible. You don't hear Christian people saying, I believe the Bible is the word of God and the word of humans—but that is what they should be saying according to the most orthodox Christian doctrine. (2) It empowers people to take any and every part of the Bible as valid for them and others, as binding on the Christian conscience (even though most of the Bible was not written by Christians), and as a touchstone of the genuineness of the Christianity of others.

I shall be heard, I know it, as denying that the Bible is the word of God. What I think I am denying is that 'word of God' is a very good description of the Bible—which is quite a different matter.

5. Then there is the concept of the 'authority' of the Bible. That term too is ripe for reconsideration. It is not that the Bible does not have force or suasive power; the question is whether the concept of authority is something the church wants to align itself with any more. The idea of the Bible's 'authority' is at home in a world where the Bible was regarded as an arsenal of prooftexts for theological warfare, and where having a scripture for it, having authorization for one's beliefs and actions, was all-important. My point is: the authority of the Bible is not the point. The authority of a text has to do with its nature; the church needs to be saying things about the Bible that have to do with its *function*. The church should be saying, not so much that the Bible is right, but that it impacts for good upon people—if that is what it believes. Perhaps it needs to recognize that 'authority' is a concept from the male world of power-relations, and that a more inclusive human language of influence, encouragement and inspiration would be more appropriate.

6. Then, while I am about it, there is the idea of the Bible as 'revelation'. Even if you want to say something very positive and strong about the Bible as originating from God, this is singularly inappropriate and misleading terminology, in my opinion. Things that are 'revealed' have formerly been hidden; but in what sense is that true about Proverbs or the Gospel of Mark? Perhaps it means that the Bible is God's revelation of his will to humanity at large? Then in what sense are the speeches of Job's friends that kind of 'revelation', and would it not surprise Luke to be told that that was what he was doing when he thought he was writing an orderly account for Theophilus of the things of which he had been informed?

7. The church needs some new language for speaking about the Bible. It needs a language of function rather than ontology. It needs to be conceiving the Bible as an agent of human transformation rather than as a rule-book. It ought to be restating its beliefs about the Bible in terms of stories and narratives of how people have been affected or changed by the Bible for the better.

8. The church needs to recognize the Bible as a heritage, a tradition, and ask how ethical people deal with a tradition. It is, strictly speaking, irresponsible to simply accept a tradition; it is an abdication of personal decision-making. It is no defence in a war crimes tribunal to say you were acting under orders; it is no defence to a charge of unethical behaviour to say you were obeying the Bible. A tradition is something that explains how you have got to where you are now; but a tradition is also a point of departure. And it must be departed from, altered, and argued with if it is going to stay alive. If it is your tradition, you cannot ignore it; that is what it means to say, It is my tradition. But there are many things you can do with a tradition besides ignoring it; and the church needs a repertory of moves that can be made with the Bible apart from swallowing it.

9. The church needs to regard the Bible as the object of theological reflection rather than as its arbiter. That it is a classic source of Christian theology is beyond question; but that does not make it its judge, its controller or its legitimator.

10. The church should admit to having an uncomfortable relationship with the Bible.[5]

4. *An End-User Theory of Interpretation*

In this section I want to propose a model for biblical interpretation that accepts the realities of our pluralist context. I call it by various names: a goal-oriented hermeneutic, an end-user theory of interpretation, a market philosophy of interpretation, or a discipline of 'comparative interpretation'.[6] This framework has two

5.   I concur heartily with the subtitle of Robert Carroll's book (as with much else in it): The Bible as a Problem for Christianity.

6.   I have presented these thoughts already in 'Possibilities and Priorities of Biblical Interpretation in an International Perspective', *Biblical Interpretation: A Journal of Contemporary Approaches* 1 (1993), pp. 67-87, and in 'A

axes: (1) the indeterminacy of meaning; (2) the authority of the interpretative community.

1. First comes the recognition that texts do not have determinate meanings. Whatever a text may mean in one context, it is almost bound to mean something different in a different context. 'Bus stop' will mean one thing when attached to a pole at the side of the road, another thing when shouted by an anxious parent to a child about to dash into that road. We may go further. Nowadays we are recognizing that texts not only do not have determinate meanings, they do not 'have' meanings at all. More and more, we are coming to appreciate the role of the reader, or the hearer, in the making of meaning, and recognizing that, without a reader or a hearer, there is not a lot of 'meaning' to any text. The text means whatever it means to its various readers, and if their contexts are different, it is likely that it will mean different things to different readers. There is no one authentic meaning which we must all try to discover, no matter who we are or where we happen to be standing.[7]

2. The second axis for my framework is provided by the idea of interpretative communities.[8] If we ask who it is that authorizes or legitimates an interpretation, who it is that says something may count as an interpretation and not be ruled out of court, the answer can only be: some group, some community, some collective that is in the business of counting and that holds court, ruling interpretations in or out. Solipsistic interpretations may be fun for their inventors, but if there is no group who will accept them, they don't survive. Some interpretations are authorized by our professional societies, some by the ecclesiastical community, but most by little sub-groups within these communities.

World Founded on Water (Psalm 24): Reader Response, Deconstruction and Bespoke Interpretation', in J. Cheryl Exum and David J.A. Clines (eds.), *The New Literary Criticism and the Hebrew Bible* (Journal for the Study of the Old Testament Supplement Series, 143; Sheffield: JSOT Press, 1993), pp. 79-90.

7.   See also my article, 'Varieties of Indeterminacy', in *Textual Indeterminacy, Part Two* (ed. Robert C. Culley and Robert B. Robinson) = *Semeia* 63 (1995), pp. 17-27.

8.   See Stanley E. Fish, *Is There a Text in This Class? The Authority of Interpretive Communities* (Cambridge, MA: Harvard University Press, 1980).

What we call legitimacy in interpretation is really a matter of whether an interpretation can win approval by some community or other. There is no objective standard by which we can know whether one interpretation or other is right; we can only tell whether it has been accepted. What your community decides counts as a reasonable interpretation of a text *is* a reasonable interpretation, and until my community decides that my interpretation is acceptable, it *isn't* acceptable. There are no determinate meanings and there are no universally agreed upon legitimate interpretations.

If there are no 'right' interpretations, and no validity in interpretation beyond the assent of various interest groups, biblical interpreters have to give up the goal of determinate and universally acceptable interpretations, and devote themselves to producing interpretations they can sell—in whatever mode is called for by the communities they choose to serve.

This is what I call 'customized' interpretation. Like the 'bespoke' tailor, who fashions from the roll of cloth a suit to the measurements and the pocket of the customer, a suit individually ordered or bespoken, the bespoke interpreter has a professional skill in tailoring interpretations to the needs of the various communities who are in the market for interpretations. There are some views of biblical texts that the church will 'buy' and 'wear', and others that only paid-up deconstructionists, footloose academics and other deviants will even try on for size.

There is nothing unethical (or novel) in cutting your garment not only according to your cloth but also according to your customer's shape. Even in a market economy, no one will compel you to violate your conscience, though it may cost you to stick to your principles. As a bespoke interpreter responding to the needs of the market, I will be interested, not so much in the truth, not at all in universally acceptable meanings, but in identifying shoddy interpretations that are badly stitched together and have no durability, and I will be giving my energies to producing attractive interpretations that represent good value for money.

In such a task interpreters of today do not have to start from scratch. For this programme has a green angle too. It is ecologically sound, because it envisages the recycling of old waste interpretations that have been discarded because they have been thought to have been superseded. In this task of tailoring to the needs of the various interpretative communities, interpreters can be aided by the array of interpretations that have already been offered in the course of the history of the interpretation of the Bible. In fact, what has usually been called the 'history of interpretation' is ripe for being reconceived as a discipline of 'comparative interpretation', providing raw materials, methods, critiques and samples for the work of designing intelligible and creative interpretations for end-users. For too long the interpretations of the past have been lumped together under the heading of the 'history' of interpretation, with the unspoken assumption that what is old in interpretation is out of date and probably rotten and the hidden implication that what is new is best. Why not rather imagine that what has been happening in the history of interpretation is that we have been stocking the shelves of the interpretational supermarket? Fashion being what it is, some day the interpretations of the past will come again into their own. I foresee, for example, a new lease of life for christological interpretations of the Old Testament, not pre-critical any longer (for we can't turn the clock back), but post-critically serving the pietism of the new Christian communities.

The biblical interpreter, in short, is in the business of serving some community or other, of meeting the needs of some group who will pay for the services biblical criticism can offer. Customers will not always know what they want, what serves their best interests, or how what they want can be correlated with what they know. Providers of a service are often in a better position than customers to make recommendations, because they know what services and facilities are available. But in the end it is the customer who will determine whether the service and the goods are acceptable or not. Those who pay the piper get to call the tune. And biblical interpreters are, from this point of view, no more than pipers, playing their tunes in the service of some community or other that authorizes their work and signs their salary cheques. Whether these biblical interpreters are state officials, preparing their students to take up their roles and duties in a capitalist society, or servants of the church, ultimately answerable to their religious community for their views and teachings, and sackable if they do not conform with the expectations of their

community, they are all working to order. Happy are those interpreters who can think what they like and say what they please
and have found a publisher who doesn't care about the market.
But what a rare breed they are!

Just to show what I have in mind by reconceiving the history of
interpretation as a science of comparative interpretation, I would
like to present some samples of historic Christian interpretation
of the last verses of Psalm 24, the entry of the King of Glory
through the ancient gates.

By way of preface, let us suppose—as all the modern commentaries would have us do—that in ancient Israelite times the poem
celebrated the transfer of the Ark to Jerusalem for the first time,
or perhaps, accompanied an annual ritual in which the Ark, sym-
bolizing the presence of Yahweh, was taken out of the city and
then restored to the temple amid festal rejoicing.[9] But we are not
living in ancient Israelite times! If the end-users of today are, for
example, Christians of the last decade of the twentieth century, I
cannot blame them if they say, Who wants to know this? Must
these contemporaries of yours and mine, who want to use this
psalm, be compelled to care so much about ancient Israelites,
dead every one of them, that they must forever read this psalm,
in their own Bible for which they paid good money, as somehow
belonging more to dead Hebrews than to live Christians?

Are these live Christians reading this psalm not entitled to ask,
Who for me is the King of Glory? What have these words to do
with me and with the central figure of the Christian faith? And
are they not also entitled to say, And if you, professional interpreter of the Old Testament, cannot tell me that, or if you think
my question illegitimate, will you kindly tell me what you are
doing with my money from the church collection plate? I have to
admit that these hypothetical rumbustious Christians have a
point. The text belongs to them too—so long as they have
acquired it legitimately and have not been robbing church
bookstalls.

---

9.   See, for example, J.H. Eaton, *Psalms: Introduction and Commentary*
(Torch Bible Commentaries; London: SCM Press, 1967), pp. 79-81; Hans-
Joachim Kraus, *Psalms 1–59: A Commentary* (trans. Hilton C. Oswald;
Minneapolis: Augsburg, 1988), pp. 312-13.

Now Christians know, especially when they are in reflective or celebratory moods—which is the atmosphere of the Psalms—that the King of Glory is Jesus Christ (whatever some dead Israelite poet, who no longer has copyright on his poem, thought). So the question becomes, not Who is the King of Glory?, for these readers know the answer to that, but To what moment in the history of the King of Glory, aka Jesus Christ, do these words attach themselves?

Enter the history of interpretation. Or rather, since it's a matter of comparative interpretation, let's go shopping. J.M. Neale, in his *Commentary on the Psalms: From Primitive and Mediaeval Writers*,[10] has seven interpretations on offer, but two of them will do for the present.

Most common in the Latin church was the view that in this psalm the gates that must lift up their heads are the gates of Hades, which Christ triumphantly enters in his descent into hell, in the days between his death and his resurrection.

In the *Gospel of Nicodemus* (not later than the mid-fourth century CE), for example, we are imaginatively transported to the scene at hell gate. Satan, who has successfully had Jesus crucified, now expects to keep him fast bound in the underworld. The personified Hades, however, is afraid of the arrival of Jesus, since he knows of the raising of Lazarus, and fears that Jesus may now be about to perform a similar miracle on all the inhabitants of the underworld. Thereupon, we read, 'a loud voice like thunder sounded: "Lift up your gates, O rulers [which is how the Vulgate reads it], and be lifted up, O everlasting doors, and the King of Glory shall come in"'. Hades replies, 'Who is this King of Glory?', and the voice sounds again, 'The Lord strong and mighty, the Lord mighty in battle'. The gates and bars of hell are suddenly crushed, the King of Glory enters hell in human form, Satan is bound in chains, while Adam, the patriarchs, the prophets and the martyrs ascend to heaven following Jesus. Hell has been harrowed.[11]

---

10. J.M. Neale and R.F. Littledale, *A Commentary on the Psalms: From Primitive and Mediaeval Writers and from the Various Office-Books and Hymns of the Roman, Mozarabic, Ambrosian...and Syriac Rites* (4 vols.; London: Joseph Masters, 1860–74).

11. *The Gospel of Nicodemus*, also known as *The Acts of Pilate*, Part II, ch. 5

Another interpretation sees here, not the harrowing of hell, but the ascension of Christ. The gates become the gates of heaven, the voices are of angels addressing one another, the King of Glory is ascending to the heavenly Mt Zion, and the scene is one of welcome. Says Augustine in his interpretation of the psalm:

> 'The heavenly spirits beheld Christ all-glorious with his wounds; and bursting into admiration at those glittering standards of divine virtue, they poured forth the hymn, *Quis est iste Rex Gloriae?* They called him not King of Glory because they saw him glorious, but because they saw him wounded.[12]

Excellent interpretations, both of them—the Gospel of Nicodemus's because it transforms the dialogue at the gate from a merely rhetorical device into a dramatic confrontation, Augustine's because he denatures and Christianizes the martial 'glory' of the psalm. But I praise them not just because they are good in themselves, of enduring quality (though I must say the harrowing of hell has gone a little out of fashion these days). What I especially like about them is that they are different, not monolithically unified.

Church interpreters, we see, have worked with the idea of a plurality of interpretations. Not for them a determinate meaning that rules out all others; rather, the text is for them, in Umberto Eco's phrase about texts in general,[13] a machine for generating interpretations, new interpretations, fresh interpretations. If the church needs anything from the Academy, it needs to be put in touch with its own exegetical tradition—which is still alive at the grass roots level, but which is frowned upon by the church

(21) (ch. 7 [23] in the Latin B text); see Montague Rhodes James, *The Apocryphal New Testament* (Oxford: Clarendon Press, 1924), p. 132.

12. Augustine, *Aurelii Augustini opera*. Pars 10. *Enarrationes in Psalmos* (ed. Eligius Dekkers and Iohannes Fraipont; Corpus Christianorum, Series Latina, 38; Turnhout: Brepols, 1956); Augustine, *Expositions on the Book of Psalms* (Nicene and Post-Nicene Fathers of the Christian Church, ed. Philip Schaff, 1/8; New York: The Christian Literature Co., 1888).

13. But I cannot find where. Was it in his *Interpretation and Overinterpretation* (with Richard Rorty, Jonathan Culler and Christine Brooke-Rose; ed. Stefan Collini [Cambridge: Cambridge University Press, 1992])? Certainly that is where he says that 'a text is a device conceived in order to produce its model reader' (p. 64).

authorities and Bible dictionary and commentary writers, in the
interests of a supposed objective exegesis. Why not say that the
church has never been interested in objective exegesis of the
scriptures, but always in how the congregations can benefit from
the scriptures. That is what has been meant by calling the Bible
the Word of God, though sadly that term has more recently
degenerated into a slogan for the supposed authority or power
of the Bible (I will return to this point soon). Those biblical interpreters who are interested in serving the church as an end-user
of their scholarship could hardly do better than appeal to the history of Christian exegesis, which for the most part has not been
constrained by the practices of the Academy. And when I say the
history of Christian exegesis I mean to include its first, scintillat-
ing example—the New Testament. When it uses the Old Testament, it gives no regard to the historical-critical meaning of
Old Testament psalms or prophecies, for example, but relates
everything to the circumstances and needs of the earliest Christian communities.[14] If the church feels uncomfortable with the
New Testament's use of the Old, it is only because the church
has subscribed to the ideals of an 'objective' academic scholarship according to which a text means one thing and one thing
only and means only what its author intended it to mean. The
New Testament knew better, and the church—I would say—
would do well to get in touch again with its roots.

4. *Worked Examples of the Bible and the Church*

On the whole, this lecture has been rather abstract and tending
towards the general. Before I conclude, I would like to offer a couple of concrete examples of how I see the problematic of the Bible
and the church.[15] Their tendency is quizzical, not doctrinaire.

14. I always set as an essay title for my course on the Psalms, 'The Use of
Psalm 2 in the New Testament', not only because it is interesting in itself
that the New Testament applies the psalm severally to the birth, the resurrection and the ascension of Jesus, as well as also to the individual
Christian, but because in so doing it implicitly poses the question of determinate exegesis.
15. The original context of these examples is my paper, 'God in the Pentateuch', in Robert L. Hubbard, Jr, Robert K. Johnston and Robert P. Meye
(eds.), *Studies in Old Testament Theology: Historical and Contemporary Images of*

1. *God and the Exodus*

In the Bible, the exodus of Israel from Egypt is represented as a great act of deliverance on God's part. The day of the exodus is called the day when 'the Lord brought you out from there by strength of hand' (Exod. 13.3), and the moment of victory over the Egyptians is recalled as the time when 'horse and rider he has thrown into the sea' (15.21). It is to be commemorated in time to come as the day when 'By strength of hand the Lord brought us out of Egypt, from the house of slavery' (13.14). Bible readers are convinced that it is telling of a mighty deed of salvation.

What the text never says, in this connection, is that it was the Lord who brought the family of Jacob into Egypt in the first place. In the book of Exodus, the presence of the Hebrews in Egypt is regarded as a given, and the only questions are whether, how and when the Lord will remove them from the house of bondage. The story of the exodus begins only at the point when the Hebrews groan under their hard labour. Then the Lord remembers his covenant with Abraham, Isaac and Jacob (Exod. 2.23-24)—which is to say, the narrative of Genesis / 12–36. No one in Exodus, in other words, seems to remember the events of Genesis 37–50, chapters that have told us how the Hebrews happen to be in Egypt in the first place; and no one seems to remember Joseph's words to his brothers, 'So it was not you who sent me here, but God' (Gen. 45.8), and 'Even though you intended to do harm to me, God intended it for good' (50.20). It is apparently not only the new Egyptian king who knows not Joseph (Exod. 1.8), but the narrator also. And his character God seems to regard the presence of the Hebrews in Egypt as nothing more than an unfortunate accident that has happened to them; he never acknowledges that it is his own deliberate design.

I myself think that it makes a difference whether the deliverance from Egypt is a sheer act of divine grace in conformity with the covenant to the forefathers, or whether it is a way of undoing the damage done to the Hebrew people by engineering their descent into Egypt in the first place. But what happens when I make the point I have just been making is that people laugh and fidget. They can see the irony of the situation, but they don't

God and God's People (Festschrift for David L. Hubbard; Dallas: Word Books, 1992), pp. 79-98.

know how to handle the fact that the Bible systematically represents this important event in a way that we would call being economical with the truth.

2. *God and the Chosen People*

It is fundamental for the Bible as a whole that God has chosen the people of Israel from among all the nations on earth. The idea first becomes apparent in Genesis 12, though the language of choosing is not yet used. When the Lord tells Abram that he will make of him a great nation and that he will bless him and make his name great (12.2), he does not say that he will *not* make other men into ancestors of great nations, that he will *not* bless them or make their name great—but he implies it. The blessing to Abram has to be preferential and competitive or otherwise Abram's significance for the 'families of the earth' (12.3) is unintelligible. God is the God of the Hebrews, God of the Hebrews in a way he is not God of the Egyptians or Hittites, for example (even if he is God of those nations in any sense at all).

This is all right if you happen to be an Israelite and have no dealings with Hittites. You know all you need to know, which is that Yahweh is your God. But if you happen to be a Hittite, or even a twentieth-century Christian reader of the Bible, is it not a problem to encounter in its pages a deity who is bound in this way to just one nation? What is the sense in this arrangement, what rationale is offered for it—especially since the Bible regards God as the creator of the whole world? The Bible itself sees no problem here, nothing to be excused or justified; if anything, it makes a point out of there being *no* rationale for the choice of Israel as the people of God. But it does not occur to it that the very idea that there should be just one nation that is the chosen people—leaving the rest of humanity unchosen—is itself problematic.

How can we modern readers of the Bible cope with the fact that the God represented in the Bible is a national deity? If you adopt the point of view of the Egyptians or the Canaanites, God is not experienced as a saving God, and the only words you will hear addressed to you are words of reproach and threat. If you are not Israel, you do not know the presence of God, and the main reason is not some defect in you but the fact that you have not been chosen. To be sure, the God of the Bible saves Israel from Egypt, but it is equally true that the same God destroys or humiliates the Egyptians, and ignores almost everyone else. The text does not wish us to think that, or, if it allows us to know it, it wants us to suppress that knowledge and concentrate on the deliverance of Israel. But when the deliverance of Israel is effected precisely through the destruction of the Egyptian soldiers, wherein lies the value of the Bible for the church?

5. *In Place of a Conclusion*

Where, you may well ask, is the positive note in all of this? What have you got to take home with you? And where, I am sure you are thinking, is the balance in all of this lecture of mine? Is this all that can be said about the Bible, that it is a bit of a headache for the church, and that most of the things the church has been saying about the Bible are wrong in some way or another?

I'm sorry, but it's not in me to end on upbeat notes, or to care about comfortable conclusions. There are plenty who do, and I'm not needed for that work. And I can't undertake balance, because that would put me in a godlike position, weighing up one thing against another and coming to a conclusion, and I don't think the time is ripe for conclusions. I don't think the evidence is all in yet, and I don't think the church has yet begun to face the problem—which means that it is out of order to be considering solutions. Asked whether the French Revolution had been successful, Mao said it was too soon to tell. Asked how the Bible can be used to soothe the church more than trouble it, I feel myself impelled to reply: it is too soon to say.

BIBLIOGRAPHY

Abravanel, Claude, and Betty Hirshowitz, *The Bible in English Music: W. Byrd—H. Purcell* (AMLI Studies in Music Bibliography, 1; Haifa: Haifa Music Museum and AMLI Library, 1970).

Alter, Robert, *The Art of Biblical Narrative* (London: George Allen & Unwin, 1981).

Andersen, Francis I., and David Noel Freedman, *Amos: A New Translation with Introduction and Commentary* (Anchor Bible, 24A; Garden City, NY: Doubleday, 1989).

Anderson, Duncan, *The Bible in Seventeenth-Century Scottish Life and Literature* (London: Allenson, 1936).

Applegate, Hilary, 'Growbag', *The Guardian*, September 19, 1992, p. 35.

Arnold, Matthew, *On Translating Homer* (1861), in M. Arnold, *On the Classical Tradition* (ed. R.H. Super; Ann Arbor: University of Michigan Press, 1960), pp. 97-216.

Arthur, Chris (ed.), *Religion and the Media: An Introductory Reader* (Cardiff: University of Wales Press, 1993).

Augustine, *Aurelii Augustini opera*. Pars 10. *Enarrationes in Psalmos* (ed. Eligius Dekkers and Iohannes Fraipont; Corpus Christianorum, Series Latina, 38; Turnhout: Brepols, 1956). *Expositions on the Book of Psalms* (Nicene and Post-Nicene Fathers of the Christian Church, ed. Philip Schaff, 1/8; New York: The Christian Literature Co., 1888).

Bar-Efrat, Shimon, *Narrative Art in the Bible* (Journal for the Study of the Old Testament Supplement Series, 70; Bible and Literature Series, 17; Sheffield: Almond Press, 1989).

Barr, David, and Nicholas Piediscalzi (eds.), *The Bible in American Education: From Sourcebook to Textbook* (The Bible in American Culture, 5; Philadelphia: Fortress Press; Chico, CA: Scholars Press, 1982).

Barr, James, *The Bible in the Modern World* (London: SCM Press, 1973).

Bauer, David R., *The Structure of Matthew's Gospel: A Study in Literary Design* (Journal for the Study of the New Testament Supplement Series, 31; Bible and Literature Series, 15; Sheffield: Almond Press, 1988).

Beeton, Isabella, *The Book of Household Management* (London: S.O. Beeton, 1861).

Bertens, Hans, *The Idea of the Postmodern: A History* (London: Routledge, 1995)

Blyton, Enid, *In the Fifth at Malory Towers* (London: Methuen, 1950).

—*The Naughtiest Girl in the School* (London: Newnes, 1940).

—*The Twins at St Clare's* (London: Methuen, 1941).

Boorstin, Daniel J., *The Image: What Happened to the American Dream* (London: Weidenfeld & Nicolson, 1961) (also published as *The Image: A Guide to Pseudo-Events in America* [New York: Atheneum, 1971]).

Brion, Marcel, and Heidi Heimann, *The Bible in Art: Miniatures, Paintings, Drawings and Sculptures Inspired by the Old Testament* (London: Phaidon, 1956).

Brittain, Victoria, 'Ghana's leader tries to buck Africa's election trend', *The Guardian*, July 4, 1992, p. 10.

Brueggemann, Walter, *The Bible and Postmodern Imagination: Texts under Negotiation* (London: SCM Press, 1993).

Buchanan, Colin, 'Not a fit state to be in', *The Guardian*, September 11, 1992, p. 19.

Carroll, Robert P., *Wolf in the Sheepfold: The Bible as a Problem for Christianity* (London: SPCK, 1991).

Casey, Paul F., *The Susanna Theme in German Literature: Variations of the Biblical Drama* (Abhandlungen zur Kunst-, Musik- und Literaturwissenschaft, 214; Bonn: Bouvier, 1976).

Childs, Brevard S., *Introduction to the Old Testament as Scripture* (London: SCM Press, 1979).

Clines, David J.A., 'A World Founded on Water (Psalm 24): Reader Response, Deconstruction and Bespoke Interpretation', in J. Cheryl Exum and David J.A. Clines (eds.), *The New Literary Criticism and the Hebrew Bible* (Journal for the Study of the Old Testament Supplement Series, 143; Sheffield: JSOT Press, 1993), pp. 79-90.

—'Beyond Synchronic/Diachronic', in Johannes C. de Moor (ed.), *Synchronic or Diachronic? A Debate on Method in Old Testament Exegesis* (Oudtestamentische Studiën, 34; Leiden: E.J. Brill, 1995), pp. 52-71.

—'Deconstructing Job', in *What Does Eve Do to Help? And Other Readerly Questions to the Old Testament* (Journal for the Study of the Old Testament Supplement Series, 94; Sheffield: JSOT Press, 1990), pp. 106-23 (originally published in Martin Warner [ed.], *The Bible and Rhetoric: Studies in Biblical Persuasion and Credibility* [London: Routledge, 1990], pp. 65-80).

—'God in the Pentateuch', in Robert L. Hubbard, Jr, Robert K. Johnston and Robert P. Meye (eds.), *Studies in Old Testament Theology: Historical and Contemporary Images of God and God's People* (Festschrift for David L. Hubbard; Dallas. Word Books, 1992), pp. 79-98.

—'Haggai's Temple, Constructed, Deconstructed and Reconstructed', *Scandinavian Journal of the Old Testament* 7 (1993), pp. 19-30 (also in Tamara C. Eskenazi and Kent H. Richards [eds.], *Second Temple Studies* [Journal for the Study of the Old Testament Supplement Series, 175; Sheffield: JSOT Press, 1993], pp. 51-78).

—'Metacommentating Amos', in Heather A. McKay and David J.A. Clines (eds.), *Of Prophets' Visions and the Wisdom of Sages: Essays in Honour of R. Norman Whybray on his Seventieth Birthday* (Journal for the Study of the Old Testament Supplement Series, 162; Sheffield: JSOT Press, 1993), pp. 142-60.

—'Possibilities and Priorities of Biblical Interpretation in an International Perspective', *Biblical Interpretation. A Journal of Contemporary Approaches* 1 (1993), pp. 67-87.

—'The Book of Psalms, where Men are Men... On the Gender of Hebrew Piety' (a preliminary version is availiable at www.shef.ac.uk/uni/academic/A-C/biblst/).

—'The Ten Commandments, Reading from Left to Right', in Jon Davies, Graham Harvey and Wilfred G.E. Watson (eds.), *Words Remembered, Texts Renewed:*

Essays in Honour of John F.A. Sawyer (Journal for the Study of the Old Testament Supplement Series, 195; Sheffield: Sheffield Academic Press, 1995), pp. 97-112 (reprinted in *Interested Parties: The Ideology of Writers and Readers of the Old Testament* [Journal for the Study of the Old Testament Supplement Series, 205; Gender, Culture, Theory, 1; Sheffield: Sheffield Academic Press, 1995), pp. 26-45).

—'Varieties of Indeterminacy', in Robert C. Culley and Robert B. Robinson (eds.), *Textual Indeterminacy, Part Two = Semeia* 63 (1995), pp. 17-27.

—*What Does Eve Do to Help? And Other Readerly Questions to the Old Testament* (Journal for the Study of the Old Testament Supplement Series, 94; Sheffield: JSOT Press, 1990).

—'Why is There a Book of Job, and What Does It Do to You If You Read It?', in *The Book of Job* (ed. W.A.M. Beuken; Bibliotheca Ephemeridum Theologicarum Lovaniensium; Leuven: Leuven University Press / Peeters, 1994), pp. 1-20.

Clines, David J.A., and Tamara C. Eskenazi (eds.), *Telling Queen Michal's Story: An Experiment in Comparative Interpretation* (Journal for the Study of the Old Testament Supplement Series, 119; Sheffield: JSOT Press, 1991).

Cockerell, Sydney C. (ed.), *Old Testament Miniatures: A Medieval Picture Book with 283 Paintings from The Creation to The Story of David* (Introduction and Legends by Sydney C. Cockerell; New York: George Braziller, n.d.).

Coggins, R.J., and J.L. Houlden (eds.), *A Dictionary of Biblical Interpretation* (London: SCM Press, 1990).

Cowper, William, *The Task, and Selected Other Poems* (London: Longman, 1994).

—*The Poetical Works of William Cowper* (ed. H.S. Milford; London: Oxford University Press, 4th edn, 1934).

Culler, Jonathan, *On Deconstruction: Theory and Criticism after Structuralism* (London: Routledge and Kegan Paul, 1983).

C.P.D., 'Weekend Birthdays', *The Guardian*, May 2, 1992, p. 28.

Eagleton, Terry, *Marxism and Literary Criticism* (London: Methuen, 1976).

Eaton, J.H., *Psalms: Introduction and Commentary* (Torch Bible Commentaries; London: SCM Press, 1967).

Eco, Umberto, *Interpretation and Overinterpretation* (with Richard Rorty, Jonathan Culler and Christine Brooke-Rose; ed. Stefan Collini; Cambridge: Cambridge University Press, 1992).

Eliot, T.S., 'Religion and Literature' (1935), in his *Selected Essays* (London: Faber & Faber, 1951), pp. 388-401.

—*Choruses from The Rock*, in T.S. Eliot, *Collected Poems 1909–1962* (London: Faber & Faber, 1974), pp. 159-85.

Exum, J. Cheryl, *Fragmented Women: Feminist (Sub)versions of Biblical Narratives* (Journal for the Study of the Old Testament Supplement Series, 163; Sheffield: JSOT Press, 1993).

Ezard, John, 'A reluctant Pope for correct English', *The Guardian*, September 12, 1992, p. 27.

Fiorenza, Elisabeth Schüssler, 'The Ethics of Interpretation: Decentering Biblical Scholarship', *Journal of Biblical Literature* 107 (1988), pp. 101-15.

Fisch, Harold, *Jerusalem and Albion: The Hebraic Factor in Seventeenth Century Literature* (New York: Schocken Books, 1964).

Fish, Stanley E., *Is There a Text in This Class? The Authority of Interpretive Communities* (Cambridge, MA: Harvard University Press, 1980).

Fitzsimons, Carmel, 'Sex, salvation and a hellfire editor', *The Guardian*, September 21, 1992, p. 25.

Fokkema, D.W., and Elrud Kunne-Ibsch, *Theories of Literature in the Twentieth Century* (London: C. Hurst & Co., 1978).

Fowl, Steve, 'The Ethics of Interpretation; or, What's Left Over after the Elimination of Meaning', in *The Bible in Three Dimensions: Essays in Celebration of the Fortieth Anniversary of the Department of Biblical Studies, University of Sheffield* (ed. David J.A. Clines, Stephen E. Fowl and Stanley E. Porter; Journal for the Study of the Old Testament Supplement Series, 87; Sheffield: JSOT Press, 1990), pp. 379-98.

Fowler, David C., *The Bible in Early English Literature* (London: Sheldon, 1977).

—*The Bible in Middle English Literature* (Seattle: University of Washington Press, 1984).

—*A History of the Bible as Literature* (2 vols.; Cambridge: Cambridge University Press, 1993).

Franks, Helen, 'Pass over the Matzos', *The Guardian*, April 18, 1992, p. 17.

Frerichs, Ernest S. (ed.), *The Bible and Bibles in America* (The Bible in American Culture, 1; Philadelphia: Fortress Press; Atlanta: Scholars Press, 1988).

Gardiner, J.H., *The Bible as English Literature* (London: T. Fisher Unwin, 1906).

Gibbs, Mary and Ellen, *The Bible References of John Ruskin* (London: George Allen, 1898).

Good, Edwin M., 'The Bible and American Music', in Giles Gunn (ed.), *The Bible and American Arts and Letters* (The Bible in American Culture, 4; Philadelphia: Fortress Press; Chico, CA: Scholars Press, 1983), pp. 129-56.

The Gospel of Nicodemus [in *The Acts of Pilate*, Part II], in Montague Rhodes James, *The Apocryphal New Testament* (Oxford: Clarendon Press, 1924).

Greeley, Andrew, 'Who says the nation is on its knees?', *The Guardian*, November 18, 1992.

Greenfield, Edward, 'Sacred origins of a sensual Salome', *The Guardian*, June 4, 1992, p. 31.

Gunn, Giles (ed.), *The Bible and American Arts and Letters* (The Bible in American Culture, 4; Philadelphia: Fortress Press; Chico, CA: Scholars Press, 1983).

Haslam, David, 'Eye of a needle', *The Guardian*, April 21, 1992, p. 20.

Hassan, Ihab, *The Postmodern Turn: Essays in Postmodern Theory and Culture* (Columbus, OH: Ohio State University Press, 1987).

Hirsch, David H., and Nehama Aschkenasy (eds.), *Biblical Patterns in Modern Literature* (Brown Judaic Studies, 77; Chico, CA: Scholars Press, 1984).

Hirsch, E.D., *Validity in Interpretation* (New Haven: Yale University Press, 1967).

Holland, Harold E., 'Fiction Titles from the Bible', *Oklahoma Librarian* 15 (1965), pp. 116-22.

Holland, Norman, *The Dynamics of Literary Response* (Oxford: Oxford University Press, 1968).

Horne, Brian, 'Poetry, English', in *A Dictionary of Biblical Interpretation* (ed. R.J. Coggins and J.L. Houlden; London: SCM Press, 1990), pp. 549-53.

Husband, Mark, 'Ghosts of civil war haunt Liberia's child soldiers. Former fighters are trying to exorcise the killing fields', *The Guardian*, April 13, 1992, p. 10.

Iser, Wolfgang, *The Act of Reading: A Theory of Aesthetic Response* (London: Routledge & Kegan Paul, 1976).

James, Montague Rhodes, *The Apocryphal New Testament* (Oxford: Clarendon Press, 1924).

Jameson, Fredric, *The Political Unconscious: Narrative as a Socially Symbolic Act* (London: Methuen, 1981).

Jauss, Hans Robert, 'Literary History as a Challenge to Literary Theory', *New Literary History* 2 (1970), pp. 7-38.

Jeffrey, David Lyle (ed.), *A Dictionary of Biblical Tradition in English Literature* (Grand Rapids: Eerdmans, 1992).

Johnson, James Turner (ed.), *The Bible in American Law, Politics, and Political Rhetoric* (The Bible in American Culture, 2; Philadelphia: Fortress Press; Chico, CA: Scholars Press, 1985).

Johns, W.E., *Biggles Defies the Swastika* (London: Oxford University Press, 1942).

—*Biggles Flies West* (London: Oxford University Press, 1937).

—*Biggles Sweeps the Desert* (London: Hodder & Stoughton, 1941).

Kahoe, W., *Book Titles from the Bible* (Moylan, PA: The Rose Valley Press, 1946).

Keenan, Brian, 'Rape', *The Guardian*, September 12, 1992, p. 9.

Klein, Lillian R., *The Triumph of Irony in the Book of Judges* (Journal for the Study of the Old Testament Supplement Series, 68; Bible and Literature Series, 14; Sheffield: Almond Press, 1988).

Kraus, Hans-Joachim, *Psalms 1–59: A Commentary* (trans. Hilton C. Oswald; Minneapolis: Augsburg, 1988).

Kreitzer, Larry J., *The New Testament in Fiction and Film: On Reversing the Hermeneutical Flow* (The Biblical Seminar, 17; Sheffield: Sheffield Academic Press, 1993).

—*The Old Testament in Fiction and Film: On Reversing the Hermeneutical Flow* (The Biblical Seminar, 24; Sheffield: Sheffield Academic Press, 1994).

Lanchester, John, 'The persuasive purist', *The Guardian*, July 2, 1992, p. 26.

Larson, Janet L., *Dickens and the Broken Scripture* (Athens, GA. University of Georgia Press, 1985).

Leveen, Jacob, *The Hebrew Bible in Art* (The Schweich Lectures, 1939; London Oxford University Press, 1944).

Lewis, C. Day (ed.), *The Collected Poems of Wilfred Owen* (London: Chatto & Windus, 1963).

Liptzin, Sol, *Biblical Themes in World Literature* (Hoboken, NJ: Ktav, 1985).

Lodge, David (ed.), *20th Century Literary Criticism: A Reader* (London: Longman, 1972).

Lyotard, Jean-François, *The Postmodern Condition: A Report on Knowledge* (trans. Geoff Bennington and Brian Massumi; Theory and History of Literature, 10; Minneapolis: University of Minnesota Press, 1984).

Marshall, Brenda K., *Teaching the Postmodern: Fiction and Theory* (New York: Routledge, 1992).

Matthews, Honor, *The Primal Curse: The Myth of Cain and Abel in the Theatre* (New York: Schocken Books, 1967).

McArthur, Tom (ed.), *The Oxford Companion to the English Language* (Oxford: Oxford University Press, 1992).

McConnell, Frank (ed.), *The Bible and the Narrative Tradition* (New York: Oxford University Press, 1986).

McCrum, Robert, 'Comrades in exile. Four emigrants to the GDR watch German capitalism dismantle all they have worked for and believed in', *The Guardian*, June 27, 1992, p. 19.

McKnight, Edgar V., *Postmodern Use of the Bible: The Emergence of Reader-Oriented Criticism* (Nashville: Abingdon Press, 1988).

Meikle, James, 'Shakespeare and Spike Milligan on original list of approved authors', *The Guardian*, September 10, 1992, p. 3.

Mitchell, Steven, and Walter Benn Michaels, 'Against Theory', in W.J.T. Mitchell (ed.), *Against Theory: Literary Studies and the New Pragmatism* (Chicago: University of Chicago Press, 1985), pp. 11-30.

Mitchell, W.J.T. (ed.), *Against Theory: Literary Studies and the New Pragmatism* (Chicago: University of Chicago Press, 1985).

Moffatt, James, *The Bible in Scots Literature* (London: Hodder & Stoughton, 1924).

[Morrison, Toni], 'A Terrible Privacy', *The Guardian*, April 18, 1992, p. 4.

Neale, J.M., and R.F. Littledale, *A Commentary on the Psalms: From Primitive and Mediaeval Writers and from the Various Office-Books and Hymns of the Roman, Mozarabic, Ambrosian…and Syriac Rites* (4 vols.; London: Joseph Masters, 1860-74).

Newnham, David, 'Paperback digest', *The Guardian*, August 22, 1992, p. 25.

Nicodemus: *see* Gospel of Nicodemus.

Nietzsche, Friedrich, *The Will to Power* (trans. Walter Kaufmann and R.J. Hollingdale; London: Weidenfeld & Nicolson, 1968 [1901]).

Nineham, Dennis, *The Use and Abuse of the Bible: A Study of the Bible in an Age of Rapid Cultural Change* (Library of Philosophy and Religion; London: Macmillan, 1976).

Noble, Richmond, *Shakespeare's Biblical Knowledge and Use of the Book of Common Prayer* (London: SPCK, 1935).

Norris, Christopher, *Deconstruction: Theory and Practice* (London: Methuen, 1982).

Parish, Steve, 'Face to Faith: A sermon on hell for John Patten', *The Guardian*, May 16, 1992, p. 26.

Phy, Stuart Allene (ed.), *The Bible and Popular Culture in America* (The Bible in American Culture, 3; Chico, CA: Scholars Press, 1985).

Platt, Steve, and Julia Gallagher, 'From Bevan to the Bible', *New Statesman and Society*, September 30, 1994, pp. 22-24.

Pryce, Robert, 'Soccer Diary', *The Guardian*, April 25, 1992, p. 16.

Pugh, Deborah, 'World's oldest book is unveiled', *The Guardian*, September 14, 1992, p. 8.

Radford, Tim, 'Babylon belittled by brothers' pi in the sky', *The Guardian*, August 29, 1992, p. 6.

Réau, Louis, *Iconographie de l'art chrétien*. Tome II. *Iconographie de la Bible*. I. *Ancien Testament* (Paris: Presses Universitaires de France, 1956).

Richards, Kent Harold, 'From Scripture to Textuality', *Semeia* 40 (1987), pp. 119-24.

Ricoeur, Paul, 'Qu'est-ce qu'un texte? Expliquer et comprendre', in R. Bubner, K. Cramer and R. Wiehl (eds.), *Hermeneutik und Dialektik. Aufsatze II. Hans-Georg Gadamer zum 70. Geburtstag* (Tübingen: J.C.B. Mohr [Paul Siebeck], 1970), pp. 181-200.

Roberts, Michael (ed.), *The Faber Book of Modern Verse* (fourth edition revised by Peter Porter; London: Faber & Faber, 1982).

Roston, Murray, *Biblical Drama in England: From the Middle Ages to the Present Day* (London: Faber & Faber, 1968).

—*Prophet and Poet: The Bible and the Growth of Romanticism* (London: Faber & Faber, 1965).

Ruthven, K.K., *Critical Assumptions* (Cambridge: Cambridge University Press, 1979).

Sandeen, Ernest R. (ed.), *The Bible and Social Reform* (The Bible in American Culture, 6; Philadelphia: Fortress Press; Chico, CA: Scholars Press, 1982).

Saussure, Ferdinand de, *Cours de linguistique générale* (1916); ET *Course in General Linguistics* (ed. Charles Bally and Albert Sechehaye in collaboration with Albert Reidlinger; London: Fontana, 1974).

Sawyer, J.F.A., 'Interpretation, History of', in *A Dictionary of Biblical Interpretation* (ed. R.J. Coggins and J.L. Houlden; London: SCM Press, 1990), pp. 316-20.

Scharlemann, Robert P., 'Theological Text', *Semeia* 40 (1987), pp. 6-19.

Scheper, G.L., 'Apple', in *A Dictionary of Biblical Tradition in English Literature* (ed. David Lyle Jeffrey; Grand Rapids: Eerdmans, 1992), pp. 49-52.

Scholes, Percy A. (ed.), *The Oxford Companion to Music* (London: Oxford University Press, 10th edn ed. John Owen Ward, 1970).

Smart, James D., *The Strange Silence of the Bible in the Church: A Study in Hermeneutics* (London: SCM Press, 1970).

Suleiman, Susan R., and Inge Crosman (eds.), *The Reader in the Text. Essays on Audience and Interpretation* (Princeton: Princeton University Press, 1980).

Tannenbaum, Leslie, *Biblical Tradition in Blake's Early Prophecies: The Great Code of Art* (Princeton: Princeton University Press, 1982).

Tawney, R.H., *Religion and the Rise of Capitalism: An Historical Study* (Holland Memorial Lectures, 1922; London: J. Murray, 1926).

Thomas, Keith, 'Great patriot who sat dazed in the ruins of the world' [review of a biography by David Cannadine], *The Guardian*, September 24, 1992, p. 24.

Tisdall, Simon, 'Disgraced mayor makes comeback', *The Guardian*, September 16, 1992, p. 8.

Tressell, Robert, *The Ragged Trousered Philanthropists* (London: Lawrence & Wishart, 1955).

Tudor-Craig, Pamela, 'Art, The Bible in', in *A Dictionary of Biblical Interpretation* (ed. R.J. Coggins and J.L. Houlden; London: SCM Press, 1990), pp. 57-65.

Tyndale, William, 'W.T. vnto the Reader', in *The New Testament Translated by William Tyndale, 1534* [a reprint of the 1534 edition] (ed. N. Hardy Wallis; Cambridge: Cambridge University Press, 1938), p. 3.

Wilby, Peter, 'Jesus beats Marx for Labour politicians', *Independent on Sunday*, September 25, 1994, p. 8.

Wimsatt, W.K., Jr, and Monroe C. Beardsley, 'The Intentional Fallacy', in W.K. Wimsatt, Jr, with Monroe C. Beardsley, *The Verbal Icon: Studies in the Meaning of Poetry* (Lexington, KY: The University Press of Kentucky, 1954, pp. 3-18).

Wodehouse, P.G., *Leave It to Psmith* (London: Barrie and Jenkins, 1924).

—*Ukridge* (London: Herbert Jenkins, 1924).

Wright, David F., Ian Campbell and John Gibson (eds.), *The Bible in Scottish Life and Literature* (Edinburgh: St Andrew Press, 1988).

Zedong, Mao, *Quotations from Chairman Mao Tse-Tung* (Peking: Foreign Languages Press, 2nd edn, 1967).

INDEX OF BIBLICAL REFERENCES

INDEX OF SUBJECTS

INDEX OF PERSONS

Lightning Source UK Ltd.
Milton Keynes UK
UKOW03f1112050913

216590UK00001B/87/A